TELECOMMUNICATIONS

SOURCE BOOKS ON EDUCATION
(Vol. 30)

GARLAND REFERENCE LIBRARY
OF SOCIAL SCIENCE
(Vol. 849)

TELECOMMUNICATIONS
A Handbook for Educators

Reza Azarmsa

GARLAND PUBLISHING, INC. • NEW YORK & LONDON
1993

Library of Congress Cataloging–in–Publication Data

Azarmsa, Reza.
  Telecommunications : a handbook for educators / by Reza
Azarmsa.
     p. cm. — (Garland reference library of social science ; vol.
849. Source books on education ; vol. 30)
  Includes bibliographical references and index.
  ISBN 0–8153–0743–8 (alk. paper)
  1. Telecommunication in education. 2. Computer networks.
3. Data transmission systems. I. Title. II. Series: Garland
reference library of social science ; v. 849. III. Series: Garland
reference library of social science. Source books on education ;
vol. 30.
LB1044.84.A94 1993
371.3'35—dc20   92–28454
                                                            CIP

Printed on acid-free, 250-year-life paper
Manufactured in the United States of America

**Dedicated to my father,
who taught me the art of communication**

Contents

Data Communications Systems 65

Acknowledgments

I would like to gratefully acknowledge the assistance of my students who read the text and provided feedback and ideas.

I wish to express my appreciation to Dr. Hossein Bidgoli, an old friend and a colleague, for reading the book proposal and making suggestions, also for his contribution to the Data Communication Security chapter. I am indebted to Mr. Clarke Sanford and Ms. Jaci Ward for their contributions to the Distance Learning chapter, and Ms. Mimi Merrill for her skillful proofreading.

I should also thank Mr. David Koeth for the charts and Mr. Lyle Williams for his creative artwork.

Many thanks to Ms. Marie Ellen Larcada, Editor, for her insightful assistance, and to Ms. Paula Ladenburg, Copy Editor, for her artful text editing.

I am very grateful to my wife, Fah, and my daughters, Vishi and Anna, who patiently and enthusiastically helped me to finish this project.

Reza Azarmsa, Ed. D.

Preface

Telecommunications is still in its infancy. A thorough treatment of recent issues seems to be imperative. The decreasing cost of hardware and software, impressive advancement in computing sophistication, and the lack of a comprehensive, up-to-date book have created a unique demand for texts in educational telecommunications.

Because telecommunications brings many benefits to society, especially to the educational community, computer experts see the 1990s as the decade of connectivity. The sharing of hardware, software, and ideas, and the cutting down of the initial investment and equipment maintenance costs has attracted educational institutions. Many now utilize telecommunications in teaching and in the learning environment.

The primary objective of this book is to provide a comprehensive introductory book on telecommunications and their applications in teaching and in the learning process. The text is enriched by concepts and applications of telecommunications in the field of education and it is aimed primarily at teachers, school administrators, and college students.

This book includes several unique features :

A) Comprehensive and up-to-date information about telecommunications. This book covers important aspects of telecommunications and its effects on society as well as education. It covers telecommunications evolution, hardware, and software and places emphasis on various facets of educational applications. The text provides the reader with comprehensive information necessary to survive in today's high-tech society.

B) In-depth, up-to-date discussion of computer networking. The decade of the '90s is known as the decade of telecommunications and computer networking. Educational institutions are rapidly joining the computer networking camp. Computer networking can bring the world into the classroom and make a student's desk a delta for information flow. Its use can improve critical thinking skills and help students to reevaluate concepts that may ultimately lead to a true global education. Network systems such as electronic mail, electronic bulletin board, and computer conferencing could be used in an educational environment to connect students, teachers, and school administrators across the districts, states, nation, or around the world. This section offers a basic understanding of networking.

C) An encyclopedic discussion on teleconferencing. Teleconferencing has expanded the horizon of education. Attention is being directed to teleconferencing as a possible way of delivering instructional materials to students in a cost-effective way. The new technology presents information in a more concrete fashion and provides students with more accurate verbal and visual facsimiles.

D) Comprehensive up-to-date discussion of distance learning. Teletraining has recently been implemented in learning environments. However, current application of telelearning is already making it possible for educational institutions to include the home or office as learning centers. Many studies have proven the validity of distance learning in the teaching/learning process.

E) Comprehensive discussion of the latest computer security for schools. Information is the most valuable asset owned by any organization. In a school, information may range from students' data to inventory data or even to sensitive students' grades. This very expensive resource can be the target of unauthorized use such as divulging the students' record, changing the students' grades, and possible destruction of school data files which would be disastrous for the school and school administrators.

More schools are becoming heavily involved in the networking environment. Security problems are much more prevalent within the network environment. In this chapter the subject of computer security for schools is discussed and some preventive measures are presented.

Not only has this book been reviewed by several of my colleagues, but feedback has been very positive, encouraging me to pursue the project further. The book material has also been field tested in many classes, and the results were satisfactory.

This book is a comprehensive educational telecommunications book and addresses issues in telecommunications such as: An Overview of Telecommunications, History of Telecommunications, Understanding Telecommunications Systems, Data Communications Systems, Networking, Computer-Mediated Communications, Teleconferencing, Distance Learning, Designing a Network System, Telecommunications Management, and Data Communication Security.

Reza Azarmsa, Ed. D.

Chapter One

An Overview of Telecommunications

Introduction

During the last five centuries, technology has revolutionized communications. From the first printing press to modern computer technology, developments in communications have constantly changed human society. Instantaneous communication around the globe, once a dream, is a reality. The ongoing communications revolution has brought us to the brink of a science-fiction future.

Rapid communications has done much to alter the structure of society. Arthur Clarke, the author of *2001: A Space Odyssey* and *2010: Odyssey Two*, believes that the communications revolution affects the way we think, work, play, do business, and relate to one another. The concept of a "global family," "electronic village," or the "universal village," through communications technology, now links nations electronically.

Electronic meetings, convened across a nation or around the world, can be beneficial as well as cost effective. Every day hundreds of teleconferences are held in different sites. Every day, thousands of interested groups share information, asking questions via telephone line, eliminating the need to travel a long distance or, in some instances, even to leave the office. Soon after the first communication satellite, Telstar 1, was launched into geosynchronous orbit in July 1962, a multi-billion dollar industry began.

Whaf Is Telecommunicafions?

Telecommunications is defined as a process of transmitting information over a distance by an electrical or electromagnetic system. This information may take the form of voice, data, image, or message. Electromagnetic transmission systems include telephone lines, cables, microwaves, satellites, and light beams.

Voice communication is known as *telephony*. Voice communication systems transmit spoken words over telephone networks in the form of electrical energy that varies in amplitude with the sound variations being transmitted. These systems include public and private, local and long distance services.

Data communications is the transmission of data from a computer in one location to another computer in other location. The data is transmitted in coded form over electrical transmission facilities.

Written message systems such as Telex send messages in data form, i.e., telegram and teletypewriter. They are message systems because they are used to transmit messages rather than conversation. Message systems provide a faster alternative to the postal service.

Image or **facsimile (FAX)** systems transmit text, pictures, diagrams, etc., via a telecommunication system to a remote location where a hard copy of the transmitted material is reproduced.

Telematics is described as merging of telecommunications with computers and television. The word *compunication* describes the same meaning. The marriage of telecommunications and computer technology has made the information age possible. The marriage has produced a number of offspring, including teleconferencing, telemarketing, telecommuting, telejournalism, telemedicine, and telelearning.

Telecommunications and Society

Telecommunications evolved as a branch of electronics, specifically, electrical engineering. As with most disciplines, electronics has its own special language. The technical aspects of the language, oriented toward electrical circuitry, often deter laypeople from studying telecommunications. However, the increasing use of electronic information handling has made it necessary for business persons—and many others as well—to understand the terminology and underlying principles of telecommunications.

Recognizing the need for people to be familiar with computers, many schools and colleges are requiring students to develop computer literacy. Telecommunications is no less important. As we progress toward "the paperless office," "the cashless society," and "the home office," persons from all walks of life are finding that a knowledge of the language and concepts of telecommunications is becoming a must. The intention of this textbook is to describe the basic terminology and concepts of telecommunications in nontechnical language so that persons with no special training or background in the field can understand them.

Modern society is rapidly becoming an information-based society, and telecommunications is central to this development. The availability of nearly "instant information" made possible by telecommunications technology is changing our jobs, our business organizations, our schools, and our personal lives.

Newspapers, threatened by increased competition and decreased profits and readership, are searching for new ways to attract and retain readers and advertisers as the print media move, however timorously, into the increasingly electronic decades of the information age. Newspapers are trying to take advantage of new communications technologies and use information they gather every day at great expense and now use only once. They want to cement a seven-day-a-week relationship with readers by becoming more useful and more interesting to a generation accustomed to the accessibility and excitement of television, computers, and video games. With the help of telecommunications technology, newspapers want to reverse a decline in the numbers of Americans reading a newspaper every day.

Many experts in communications technology envision a personalized electronic newspaper available by some combination of computer and television set, early in the next century; in the meantime, some newspapers are experimenting with a variety of intermediate technologies. More than a dozen newspapers have tried sending small editions to selected subscribers by FAX, and others are experimenting with various versions of videotex—newspapers by computer.

For example, *Rocky Mountain News*, published in Denver, Colorado, gives subscribers the computer software necessary to receive—free of charge—a separate edition of the daily paper, updated frequently and available 24 hours a day by computer-telephone hookup.

The *Fort Worth Star-Telegram*, published in Texas, another daily newspaper, offers stories from the daily paper and from national news services to the residents on StarText—a computer service that enables users to get an early look at the next day's classified ads, as well as make travel reservations, exchange electronic messages, and access a "reference room" that includes book and movie reviews and gardening tips via telephone line. The *Atlanta Journal* and *Atlanta Constitution* have 250 special telephone lines for readers who want sports scores, news updates, restaurant reviews, movie schedules, soap opera updates, and stock, weather, and traffic reports.

Many newspapers have established 900 telephone numbers that require users to pay a fee for recorded information. The callers can get information on stock market reports, crossword puzzle clues, horoscopes, weather reports, restaurant reviews, soap opera updates, sports scores, recipes, as well as travel, entertainment, and real estate information.

Telecommunications in Business Organizations

Information is the lifeline of modern business; it provides the basis for all business activities. Managers apply judgment to the information available to make their decisions—decisions that have a strong impact upon the success of any enterprise. Recognizing their dependency upon information, businesses have begun to focus on the management of this vital resource.

The present trend in information management is to establish formal *management information systems (MIS)* to make information immediately available to various levels of management throughout an organization. Some companies have created separate Management Information System Departments to coordinate the flow of information throughout the organization. Telecommunications plays a key role in these departments.

Telecommunications makes possible the technique of *distributed processing,* which links intelligent terminals to central computer processing facilities through the use of communication lines. Telecommunications also makes possible the instant availability of information from a centralized database (facts arranged in computer files for access and retrieval) within an organization. With a database, information can be shared among the various departments of an organization and among remotely located branches. Thus, many different people with different job responsibilities can access the database from terminals, often referred to as *workstations,* located in their work areas.

Some companies have established industry-wide databases that can be accessed from virtually anywhere via telecommunication lines. Companies that maintain database services offer access to their database for a subscription fee. These information centers are available for many industries and professions, including transportation, banking, investments, publications, law, and medicine. The databases are protected from unauthorized access by security measures that require user identification via a password or series of passwords.

WESTLAW, one commercial database system, was created by West Publishing Company, a publisher that has served the legal profession for over a century. The WESTLAW system connects remote terminals located in law offices, courts, and government agencies with a centralized database by means of telephone lines. Users enter commands or inquiries at a typewriter-like keyboard; responses are displayed on the cathode ray tube (CRT), or terminal screen. Users can record information appearing on the screen on paper by means of an associated printer. The system is protected from unauthorized access by a multistep sign-on procedure.

This system offers legal research capabilities that permit a lawyer to scan large numbers of cases and identify relevant ones in a few seconds. The system has two basic advantages:

1. speed in finding the research material
2. search capabilities not possible using books

The system's unique search capabilities allow users to access case summaries using terms other than those indexed in law books. For example, users can locate a case by entering almost any term associated with that court decision—names of judges, witnesses, companies, and unusual nonlegal terms.

WESTLAW is constantly being updated; as new cases are reported, they are added to the database. The system has improved legal research by allowing users to accomplish more research in less time and by providing new search capabilities.

Many organizations are using telecommunications effectively to enhance their services or to provide new services. Additionally, there are industries whose very existence depends upon telecommunications. Among these are airlines, banking, investments, credit card services, and hotel/motel reservation systems.

Airlines

All major airlines in the United States have computerized systems for handling reservations. To make a reservation, a person dials a local telephone number that connects to a regional reservation center, probably located in a distant city. The regional center is linked to a national center by telephone lines. The reservation clerk keys in the desired destination on a remote terminal to access the central computer and obtain information about possible flights. Information displayed on the terminal screen lists the flights on which seats are available and the fares. When the traveler selects a flight, the clerk enters the details of the booking into the system, and the computer's seat inventory is updated. The cancellation of reservations also is handled automatically; the computer cancels the reservation and adds to the number of seats available on the flight. In addition, the computer keeps a waiting list of passengers desiring reservations and their telephone numbers. Reservation systems are interlinked with those of other airlines so that connecting flights can be booked.

Telecommunications also permits computer operators to monitor air traffic from control towers. A computer system identifies each approaching plane and tracks its altitude and speed, enabling air traffic controllers to give directions for landing.

Banking

Another major industry dependent upon telecommunications technology is banking. Banks use remote terminals and telecommunication lines to update customers' accounts. Tellers located either at main offices or branch offices insert the customer's passbook into a computer terminal and key in relevant information; the terminal prints the entry in the passbook and transmits the information to update the central computer files.

In some cases, customers can use their push-button telephones to perform certain banking transactions such as paying bills, transferring funds, and determining their bank balances. The telephone functions as an input terminal when it is connected to the bank's central computer by telephone lines. The user communicates with the computer by entering appropriate codes on the telephone key-pad.

Banks also use telecommunication lines to provide automatic teller service. Automatic teller terminals are connected to the bank's central computer via communication lines. To process a transaction, the customer inserts an identifying bank card into the terminal and keys in a personal identification number. After the computer performs appropriate checks on the customer's identity and account status, the customer keys in a transaction code, and the machine completes the transaction. Automatic tellers are located in shopping malls, supermarkets, and places of employment as well as on bank premises. Many of these terminals accommodate bank cards issued by cooperating banks, credit unions, and savings and loan associations. Automatic tellers offer the convenience of 24-hour operation for the most frequently used services such as deposits, withdrawals, and payments to utilities and credit card accounts.

Many banks now participate in shared networks: a bank network system in one area of the country interconnects to another bank network in another area. It should be noted that banks also have to talk between themselves. Some networks available for this type of communication are:

- SWIFT (Society for Worldwide Interbank Financial Telecommunications)
- MINTS (Mutual Institution National Transfer System)
- FED WIRE (Federal Reserve Bank Telecommunications Network)
- BANK WIRE (Interbank Network)

These networks are used for transferring information between banks. Banks also create private networks and interconnect them for use with the general public. Wholesale electronic funds transfer between banks. By contrast, private bank networks involve retail electronic funds transfer for use by the general public and/or customers of each individual bank. A bank's network for its checking/savings branch offices, ATMs, POS terminals, home banking, and the like would be their retail network.

Credit Card Service

The widespread use of credit cards has resulted in the creation of a new industry to serve as a clearinghouse for credit card transactions. A major function of this service is verifying accounts to reduce fraudulent use of credit cards. When a customer presents a card to be used for payment, the merchant calls the service company to obtain a credit status report. The service company searches its computer files and reports the status of the account. Account verification is a high-speed transaction; the entire process is completed in a few seconds. The service depends upon telecommunication between a centralized database and merchants located virtually anywhere in the world.

Electronic Shopping

A recent communication growth area is electronic shopping. A company selling consumer products holds an auction on television, and the viewers at home can bid on the various products. The customers see the goods for sale on their television set and bid on or purchase them through a two-way data transmission. Although it remains to be seen whether this method of selling products over television will be satisfactory to customers in the long run, it has become quite popular, and the stock of companies providing this service has risen rapidly in value.

Insurance

Telecommunications enables insurance companies to operate more efficiently and to offer better service to their customers.

Insurance companies with millions of policyholders generally have a home office and a number of branch offices located throughout the country. Policy records are kept in a central computer located in the home office, and the branch offices are connected to the home office computer via telecommunication lines. Each branch office is equipped with a terminal that permits it to communicate with the headquarters computer. When a policyholder requests information regarding coverage, a clerk in the branch office enters the request on the terminal keyboard. The computer accesses the files and reports the requested information on the terminal screen at the branch office. The entire process takes only a few seconds; thus, the clerk is able to respond to the customer's request without delay.

Investment

Another industry that depends on the immediate communication of information is the investment business. Both the New York Stock Exchange and the American Stock Exchange—the two major stock exchanges in the country—are located in New York City. All trading of stocks they list is conducted on the floor and sell orders are transmitted over communication lines to their representatives at the stock exchange. As each transaction is completed, it is recorded on a computer and simultaneously transmitted to brokerage offices all over the country. Some brokerage offices display this information on a continuous tape, thus providing up-to-the-minute details of all trading transactions. Many brokerage offices also have display terminals connected to the New York computer. Stockbrokers use these terminals to obtain current price information on any stock from the computer. The brokerage industry relies heavily on rapid communication, since investors' trading decisions are based on the latest market prices.

Rental Car Industry

Another major application for large national and international communication networks is in the rental of automobiles. Avis Rent-A-Car was the first major company to develop an online real-time rental car network. This network interconnects the major locations where automobiles might be rented, picked up, and returned.

The networks used by rental car companies involve multiplexed circuits. These circuits are leased from the major telephone companies and/or special common carriers which sell communication circuits. A rental car network is quite similar to an airline network in that it is used to keep track of dates when cars have to be returned to their lessor, make rental agreements with customers, calculate the cost and mileage utilized, and perform other general accounting functions.

Teleconferencing

One of the growing uses for communications is in teleconferencing between the employees of a single company or those of several companies. Teleconferencing allows users to sit in a conference room and talk to another group of users in another conference room thousands of miles away. Participants are able to see and hear the other people when they speak, and the system can focus in on a specific document and allow everyone to read it at the same time. The document can even be copied at either end of the teleconferencing link. Teleconferencing also can be set up as a multipoint network in which several conference rooms in various cities are interconnected.

The primary reason for using teleconferencing is to save time and get a widely dispersed group of people together when they need to discuss a common problem. It also can save considerable amounts of money by reducing travel costs. Teleconferencing has the advantage of being able to transmit documents, pictures, charts, visuals, graphs, or anything else that can be sent over a standard television set. This topic will be discussed in detail in chapter 7.

Applications of Telecommunications in Education

Telecommunications can bring the world into the classroom and make a student's desk a delta for information flow. Properly structured and facilitated within the existing curriculum, instructional telecommunications can be a powerful tool in the instructional arsenal. It can improve critical thinking skills and help us reevaluate concepts that may ultimately lead to true global education.

Sayer and Brown (1987) reported on project Orillas to promote Spanish language literacy. In this project, local electronic bulletin boards were connected to an international network of bulletin boards to exchange ideas. Classes in Mexico and Puerto Rico were linked with bilingual classrooms of Latino students in the United States. The goal was to improve students' educational achievements, especially writing skills in the United States, where Spanish is a minority language, and in Mexico and Puerto Rico, where it is the dominant language.

Engaging students in a dialogue using telecommunications (computer-mediated dialogue) as the medium of exchange can be a motivating and enriching experience. Unlike conventional pen pals, telecommunication allows an individual student, or class of students, to discuss and share experiences with unlimited others. The physical distance between students becomes unimportant (save the cost of the telephone call), because telephone lines stretch across the country and around the world. Telecommunications has some significant advantages over the more conventional models of exchanging information. With telecommunications, an open letter to a very large audience is possible, inviting any number of responses. On-line, immediate exchanges are possible. For example, two geographically-separated classes or groups could debate the relative merits of candidates in upcoming elections. Classroom preparation before going on-line with each other might include researching candidates' positions, interviewing selected persons, uncovering biographical histories, and just about any conventional classroom activity that would otherwise surround an assignment of this nature. When the classes were fully prepared, they would go on-line and present their opinions to students in another school, district, state, or country. In support of their arguments (and taking full advantage of the medium they are employing) they might also transfer position papers or support documents they have drafted.

Electronic pen pals seem like a productive way to start out a network interaction: students are motivated, they can write for a distant audience, and they may learn about different cultures through interaction with their electronic pen pals.

A better initial activity than computer pals is to create and post a "class directory," in which students write a short description of themselves and their interests. You can post this directory on the bulletin board and then students elsewhere who read it and who have matching interests can establish contact with your students. If a cluster of common interests appears in the directory, then someone can use that as a basis for organizing a new network activity centered on that interest.

Electronic messaging is a powerful and productive educational tool. Students exchange social studies reports, book reports, poetry, short stories, mathematics problems, and scientific data.

The students begin to see themselves as readers, writers, and researchers.

Services available from the bulletin board include a calendar of events, announcements, job openings, new legislation, notice of availability of grants, education and career information, educational statistics, licensed software that may be downloaded by authorized persons, and public-domain software that may be accessed by anyone.

Network systems also make possible electronic mail systems that allow students and teachers to communicate with one another via "mailboxes" on the network.

Long-distance electronic mail gives young scientists access to the resources of experts in the outside world and provides students with wider audiences for their scientific observations and their findings. Electronic mail allows students to communicate with each other using the computer. To implement this program, all that is needed is a disk drive, a few disks, a word processing program, a modem, and at least one microcomputer. Students are able to send and receive messages on a disk. This gives students the opportunity to practice writing in order to express their ideas to each other.

An electronic message center provides students with the opportunity to write about their interests in a new and intriguing format. Furthermore, an electronic mail system creates an environment in which students must write to communicate.

Teachers can generate material for electronic mail messages by asking students for ideas. For example, reviews (critical discussions of movies, books, records or television shows), whimsy (collections of jokes, anecdotes or riddles), want ads (things to sell or things wanted), recipes (favorite recipes and comments about recipes shared), news (discussions of current events), trivia (trivia questions asked and answered), writing (poems, essays, and short stories by students), improve it (a sentence or paragraph with errors in it; students reply with a list of the errors found), stories (additions to a continually growing story), colleges (discussions of colleges and universities to visit), clubs (announcements of club meetings and activities), classes (recommendations on classes to take; discussions of class projects), and sales (information about local store sales.)

Networking may have some disadvantages. The reasons for implementing a network are sometimes overwhelmed by the cost and problems associated with its maintenance and use. Most networks require one individual who is knowledgeable about hard disk management to act as the network manager, further adding to the cost of maintaining a system. In addition, technical support by vendors is sometimes inadequate. When computer hardware, networking hardware and software, and educational software are purchased from three different vendors, it may be difficult to determine which company is in fact responsible for making a repair or fixing a software problem.

Application software that is copy-protected cannot run on a network that utilizes a hard disk/file server. That means that the majority of packages for stand-alone computers will not work on a network. Even if a networkable version is available, it may not work on the particular network installed in your school.

Network systems can be used for teacher inservice programs and professional development. Educators would be able to confer and to exchange new ideas and plans without the usual disadvantages, such as travel costs or loss of valuable work hours. They can experience these advantages all the time; unlike traditional meetings, telecommunications conferences are not just "once-a-year" events.

Being linked into the network allows the educators access to a number of useful conferences where they can exchange messages and papers at concurrent sessions, just as they would at a conference at a hotel or convention center. Unlike hotel conferences, the network users can, at any given time, participate in multiple computer conferences with participants across the nation.

Participants currently can add sessions to existing conferences or even initiate a new conference whenever the need arises. The teachers can access filed information such as certification requirements, calendars, personnel information, curriculum guides, instructional materials, and special projects on the network.

The conference capability has proved to be a powerful mechanism for administrators to plan new undertakings, to resolve problems, and to develop new policies.

Today there are veritable storehouses of electronic information, including just about everything ever published. Huge databases of information serve as online resources or libraries. These electronic libraries, housed primarily in giant mainframe computers, are often available to classrooms and educators at subscription rates. Some of the more commonly used subscription mainframe databases are Dialog, CompuServe, and GEnie. To use these databases, you must first purchase an account with the service. This is a one-time charge, but there is an ongoing cost of connecting to the service. You are charged according to the amount of time you remain connected to the mainframe.

References

Batt, Russell H. (1989). The Computer Bulletin Board. *Journal of Chemical Education*, August, A198-A201.

Brienne, Deborah and Goldman, Shelley. (1989). Networking: How It Has Enhanced Science Classes in New York Schools . . . and How It Can Enhance Classes in Your School, Too. *Classroom Computer Learning*, April, 45-53.

Coombs, Norman. (1990). Computing and Telecommunications in Higher Education: A Personal View. *Educational Technology*, February, 46-47.

Coombs, Norman. (1988). History by Teleconference. *History Microcomputer Review*, Spring, 37-39.

Gallagher, Brian. (1989). VideoTechnology: Its Effect on Teaching English and Film. *Education Digest*, March, 29-32.

Gersten, R., Carnine, D., and Woodard, J. (1987). Direct Instruction Research: The Third Decade. *Remedial and Special Education*, June, 48-56.

Hasselbring, T., Sherwood, R., Bransford, J., Fleenor, K., Griffith, D., and Goin, L. (1987). An Evaluation of the Level-One Instructional Videodisc Program. *Journal of Educational Technology Systems*, Spring, 151-169.

Hofmeister, Alan M. (1989). Teaching with Videodiscs. *Teaching Exceptional Children*, Spring, 52-54.

Kelly, Luke and Zuckerman, Michael. (1990). Telecommunications-Electronic Mail. *Journal of Physical Education, Recreation and Dance*, Spring, 86-89.

Koorland, M. A. (1990). Telecommunications Skills Training for Students with Learning Disabilities: An Exploratory Study. *Educational Technology*, January, 34-36.

Lubke, Margaret M., Rogers, Beverly, and Evans, Kim T. (1989). Teaching Fractions with Videodiscs. *Teaching Exceptional Children*, Spring, 55-56.

Meskill, C. (1987). Educational Technology Product Review: Mastering Ratios. *Educational Technology*, July, 41-42.

Miller, Susan C. and Cooke, Nancy L. (1989). Mainstreaming Students with Learning Disabilities for Videodisc Math Instruction. *Teaching Exceptional Children*, Spring, 57-60.

Petersen, L., Hofmeister, A. M., and Lubke, M. (1988). A Videodisc Approach to Instructional Productivity. *Educational Technology*, February, 16-22.

Romiszowski, Alexander and de Haas, Johan. (1989). Computer Mediated Instruction: Using E-Mail as a Seminar. *Educational Technology*, October, 7-14.

Rye, Jell-Jon. (1988). Technology Learning Activities Motivate Students. *Education Digest*, October, 49-51.

Sayers, Dennis and Brown, Kristin. (1987). Bilingual Education and Telecommunications: A Perfect File. *The Computing Teacher*, April, 23-24.

Schug, Mark C. (1988). Computers in High School Social Studies. *Education Digest*, November, 23-26.

Vlahakis, Robert. (1988). From TASS to Tallahassee: In Search of Today's News. *Classroom Computer Learning*, May/June, 82-87.

Wasson, Lynn E. (1990). Electronic Mail: Teaching It by Using It. *Business Education Forum*, January, 15-17.

Chapter Two

History of
Telecommunications

Introduction

At the beginning, communication over long distance was very limited. Making fire and smoke, sounding a drum, shouting or screaming, hand signals, etc. were used. On many occasions, runners or horses were used to deliver a message over the distance. Pony express, the great American tradition, was a good example. As we all know, pigeons were reliable in early telecommunications. In 1815, the Rothschilds used carrier pigeons to track the progress of the battle of Waterloo.

In 1790, Claude Chappe built a fairly large network of semaphore stations on the hill tops in France. From a high vantage point and with a colored flag in each hand, the semaphore operators would change the position of each flag to pass messages to several receivers many miles away. It was not until the nineteenth century, however, that the electromagnetic mode of speech transmission came into use.

Morse and Telegraph

The middle of the 19th century saw the introduction of electrical telecommunications to the world. Samuel Morse, a portrait painter, sent his first telegraph message between Washington, D.C., and Baltimore, Maryland, in 1844. Morse transmitted this message "What hath God wrought." This phrase was repeated 118 years later in 1962, by John F. Kennedy when he spoke to Lagos, Nigeria, on the first transatlantic telephone call via satellite. After transmitting the message the United States postmaster general decided that the telegraph was a toy and would not be successful.

Morse formulated the principles for sending and receiving telegrams as a dot-dash-space code based on the duration or absence of electrical impulses. He developed his code by assigning dot and dash combinations to the letters of alphabet. Figure 2. 2 shows the Morse code.

Morse's development of a practical telegraph was based in part on research by other individuals. Morse, however, was the one who brought this practical device to the marketplace.

In May 1845 Morse organized Magnetic Telegraph Company, the first telegraph company in the U. S. Many telegraph stations were established. Sending a message from one point to another point was difficult because it had to be transmitted from one station to another, taking a long time.

The telegraph soon exerted a strong influence upon the political and economic life of the nation. Its impact upon railway operation and management was substantial. The telegraph provided the railroads with electric train dispatching, informing management of the location of every train on its rail system. The railroads, for their part, provided the telegraph companies with an exclusive right-of-way; telegraph wires were strung on poles

Figure 2.1. *Early tribal communications*

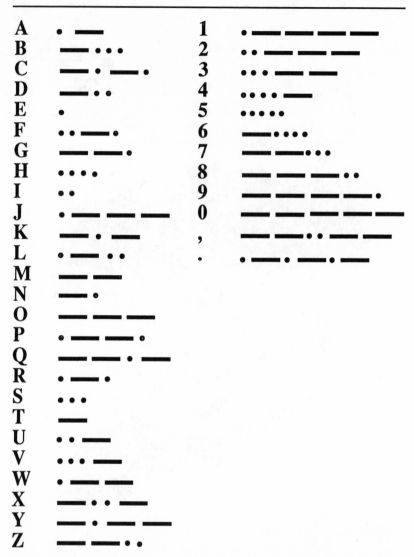

Figure 2. 2. *Morse Code consists of combinations of dots and dashes and is based on the duration or absence of electrical impulses.*

beside the railroads. Since each industry had something of value to offer the other, their service contracts with each other became valuable assets.

Another industry closely associated with the development of the telegraph was the newspaper industry. The advent of the telegraph revolutionized the collection and dissemination of news. Since the industry was dependent upon receiving and printing the news as rapidly as possible, it had to employ the only method of rapid communication available at the time—the telegraph.

By the beginning of the Civil War, telegraph lines linked most of the major cities in the nation. The war years saw a dramatic rise in the use of telegraphic communications. The military, faced with assembling troops and supplies and moving them to the battle fronts, found the telegraph invaluable. Businesses, too, deluged the telegraph offices with messages in a desperate effort to get their affairs in order before contacts between the North and the South were broken.

One of the telegraph companies whose business prospered during the war years was Western Union. Originally incorporated under the name New York and Mississippi Valley Printing Telegraph Company, the organization was reincorporated in 1856 as the Western Union Telegraph Company. With its telegraph lines located north of the Mason-Dixon line and the Ohio River, it was situated advantageously to profit from the increase in telegraph business brought about by the war.

As early as 1936 it had become quite evident that with the steady growth in telephone demand, there soon would not be enough space to house the system's switches. In 1947 William Shockley, John Bardeen, and Walter Brattain connected two wires to a chip and invented the transistor.

Western Union was the first large telecommunications company in America. The company grew rapidly and offered services to all parts of the United States. In 1943 Western Union acquired Postal Telegraph, Inc. but post-Second World War slowed down the need for telegraph and increased the demand for telephony. Western Union strengthened its position by offering teletypewriter service (Telex), private lines for voice, data, and facsimile. In 1971 Western Union purchased the Teletypewriter Exchange Service (TWX) from AT&T (American Telephone and Telegraph). In addition, it offers money orders, computer-switched teletype, and message services known as Mailgram. Western Union has two WESTAR satellites for its services and lease purposes.

Today with the telephone readily available, message communications are a low priority since the phone is two-way communication in a real time anywhere in the world.

Telephone

In 1876, Alexander Graham Bell, a teacher for deaf people, developed the telephone. His first message on the telephone was "Mr. Watson, come here. I need you."

In the summer of 1876 Bell exhibited his "speaking telephone" at the Centennial Exposition in Philadelphia. He demonstrated it to Dom Pedro, Emperor of Brazil and Sir William Thompson, British physicist (later Lord Kelvin). This demonstration was successful.

In 1877 the first Bell stock was issued and the Bell Telephone Company was formed. The Bell Company started to sell the service not the equipment, renting the equipment and keeping possession of it.

The telephone quickly eclipsed the telegraph as a means of telecommunications. While the telegraph relied on trained operators, the telephone could be used by anyone. The telegraph represented message/data communications while the telephone was voice communications.

In 1885 the American Telephone and Telegraph Company (AT&T) was formed to build long distance lines. In 1900 AT&T absorbed the American Bell Company and became the headquarter company of the Bell System. In 1909 Bell bought controlling interest in Western Union and Bell president, Theodore Vail, became president of both companies. In 1912 the independent telephone companies protested that the AT&T was violating antitrust laws. Kingsburg, vice president of AT&T, committed AT&T not to acquire additional independent telephone companies.

In 1981 the FCC ruled that computer companies can transmit data on an unregulated basis, and the Bell system was permitted to engage in data processing activities. As a result, AT&T formed a new company called AT&T Communications.

In 1982, as a result of the 1974 government antitrust lawsuit, AT&T was required to divest itself of all its operating companies, and was prohibited from using the Bell name. The operating companies were formed into seven regional corporations to provide local telephone service and its switching.

The telephone works as a result of application of a fundamental physical phenomenon: words spoken into a telephone mouthpiece are converted into electromagnetic impulses and transmitted over telephone lines. At the receiving instrument, these impulses are reconstructed into speech in such a manner that even the voice characteristics of the speaker are recognizable. This conversion phenomenon is basic not only to telephone but to the entire field of telecommunications as well.

All telephones consist of at least three parts:

The transmitter, which is similar to a microphone, converts voice vibrations into electrical impulses, which are then transmitted over telephone wire, radio waves, or satellites.

The receiver, which converts the incoming electrical impulses to sounds.

Figure 2. 3. *Bell Goes Cordless!*

The bell unit, which rings or buzzes when activated by an incoming call.

Today's modern phones have either rotary dial or pushbutton keys that allow callers to place calls directly. A switch hook signals the telephone company central office and incoming caller that the telephone is either idle or in use. When the phone is not in use, the handset rests on the base and switch hook is in the off position.

Telephone lines consist of a pair of wires. Early telephones were equipped with batteries for providing current. Each telephone had magneto. By cranking the handle on the generator, the user activated a bell or light at the operators station. The operator then connected the line to the line being called. Modern phone lines have common-battery operation, in which a central source of electricity is always available for use.

Federal Communications Commission (FCC)

In 1934 the Congress passed the Communications Act and as a result the Federal Communications Commission (FCC) was created to regulate the interstate and international communications policies for radio, television, wire, and cable. Its responsibilities include: encouraging the development and operation of broadcast and communications services at reasonable rates, regulating and licensing broadcast stations, reviewing and evaluating station performance, approving changes of ownership and major technical alterations, regulating cable television, prescribing and reviewing accounting practices, regulating and issuing licenses for all forms of two-way radio, reviewing applications of telephone and telegraph companies for changes in rates and services, setting permissible rates of return for communication common carriers, and reviewing technical specifications for new telecommunications equipment.

In 1978 the National Telecommunications and Information Administration (NTIA) was formed. Its function is to provide advisory assistance in telecommunications and information issues for the Department of Commerce in addition to formulating policies to support the development and growth of telecommunication industries, furthering the efficient development and use of telecommunications and information services, providing policy and management for federal use of electromagnetic spectrum, and providing telecommunication facilities grants to public service users.

Radio

Radio, the oldest of the telecommunications media, formed most of the models of entertainment and information that are common to the media today. Many people believe that radio originated in 1873 when James Clerk Maxwell, a physics professor at Cambridge University, England, published his theory of electro-magnetism. His *Treatise on Electricity and Magnetism* predicted the existence of radio waves and how they should behave based on his observations of how light waves behave.

Experiments to prove Maxwell's theory were undertaken by the German physics professor Heinrich Hertz during the 1880s. Hertz actually generated at one end of his laboratory and transmit-ted to the other end the radio energy that Maxwell had theorized. He thus proved that variations in electrical current could be projected into space as radio waves similar to light waves. Originally radio waves were called "Hertzian waves," and today Hertz's name is used as a frequency measurement meaning cycles per second.

A battle was waged in the 1890s between General Electric (GE) and Westinghouse over whose patent would be adopted for nationwide electrical use. GE favored direct current (DC) and Westinghouse favored alternating current (AC). In 1896 Westinghouse won the contest and AC became the national standard. Long-distance radio wave radiation is dependent on AC generation, so it is fortunate for radio that this was the adopted standard.

Guglielmo Marconi, often referred to as the "Father of Radio," expanded upon radio principles. Marconi, the son of a wealthy Italian father and an Irish mother, was scientifically inclined from an early age. Fortunately, he had the leisure and wealth to pursue his interests. Shortly after he heard of Hertz's ideas, he began working fanatically in his workshop, finally reaching a point where he could actually ring a bell with radio waves.

After he had tested his invention outside his workshop by successfully transmitting throughout his estate and beyond, Marconi wrote to the Italian government in an attempt to interest them in his project. They replied in the negative. His determined Irish mother decided that he should take his invention to England. There, in 1897, he received a patent and the financial backing to set up the Marconi Wireless Telegraph Company, Ltd. Under the auspices of this company Marconi continued to improve on wireless and began to supply equipment to ships. In 1899 he formed a subsidiary company in the United States, the Marconi Wireless Company of America. The famous transmission of the letters across the Atlantic, from Britain to Newfoundland, occurred in 1901 and was, of course, a great breakthrough for what eventually became radio.

Although Marconi maintained a dominant international position in wireless communication, many other people were experimenting and securing patents in Russia, Germany, France, and the United States. Until this time the primary use of wireless had been as a means of Morse code communication by ships at sea. Now some people were becoming intrigued with the idea of voice transmission.

A significant step in this direction was taken by John Fleming of Britain in 1904. He developed the vacuum tube, which led the way to voice transmission.

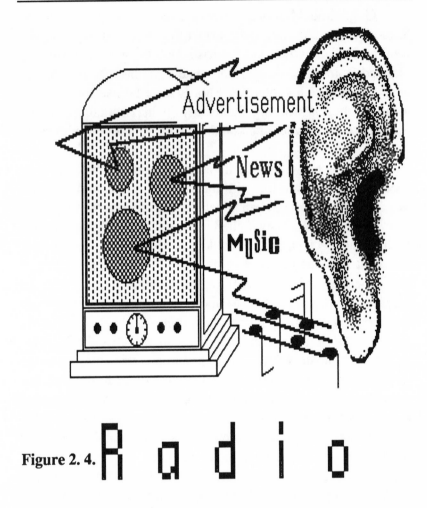

Figure 2. 4. Radio

By 1910 radio waves had been theorized by James Maxwell, proved to exist by Heinrich Hertz, put to use with Morse code by Guglielmo Marconi, and developed for voice transmission by John Fleming, Reginald Fessenden, and Lee De Forest.

At the beginning of World War I the government took over all radio operation. Ship-to-shore stations were operated by the Navy, and many ham radio operators were sent overseas to operate radio equipment so that the government could develop the transmitters and receivers needed.

As the novelty of radio wore off, performers were less eager to appear and some means of financing programming had to be found. Many different ideas were proposed, including donations from citizens, tax levies on radio sets, and manufacturer and distributor payment for operating stations. Commercials came about largely by accident.

Radio became the primary entertainment medium during the depression. In 1930, 12 million homes were equipped with radio receivers, but by 1940 this number had jumped to 30 million. During the same period, advertising revenue rose from $40 million to $155 million. In 1930 NBC-Red, NBC Blue, and CBS offered approximately sixty combined hours of sponsored programs a week. By 1940 the four networks (Mutual had been added) carried 156 hours.

The government did not take over broadcasting during World War II as it had during World War I. However, it did solicit the cooperation of radio for morale and public service announcements, bond purchase appeals, conservation campaigns, and civil defense instructions. Among the most famous of these solicitations were singer Kate Smith's marathon broadcasts for war bonds. Her appeals sold over $100 million worth of bonds. Many of the plays and soap operas produced during the period dealt with the war effort, and some even tried to deal with the segregation problem, which was coming to a head because of segregation in the armed forces. Several soap operas presented Negroes (the preferred term at that time) in esteemed professional roles.

One result of the war was the perfection of audio tape recorders. Events could now be recorded and played back whenever desired.

In the early 1930s the demand was high to eliminate *static* in radio broadcasting. Edwin H. Armstrong invented a whole new system—frequency modulation (FM). He built an experimental 50,000-watt FM station in New Jersey. In the late 1930s and early 1940s an FM bandwagon was rolling, and some 150 applications for FM stations were submitted to the FCC. As a result, the FCC altered channel 1 on the TV band and awarded *spectrum* space to FM. It also ruled that TV sound should be frequency modulated.

Today FM is a healthy medium in terms of both dollars and audience and an increasing number of FM stations have found their way to the top of the ratings charts.

A very significant recent radio event is deregulation. In 1981, the government lifted many regulations governing radio. Station licenses are now issued for seven years rather than three, and radio stations are no longer limited in the amount of commercial minutes they can program. Furthermore, radio stations are no longer required to program news and public affairs programs, and they have been relieved of ascertaining the needs of the community and of keeping program logs. In 1984, in further deregulation, the FCC increased the number of radio stations one company could own. Previous rules had limited ownership to seven AM (amplitude modulation) stations and seven FM stations, but the new rules increased this to twelve of each.

Today's radio audiences listen to stations rather than programs. This is because most stations have a "sound," which usually translates into a particular format—country and western, top-40, easy listening, religious, contemporary hits, new wave, jazz, all news, or talk. Listeners know that when they tune in a particular station, they will hear a particular sound. Because different age groups tend to prefer different sounds, each radio station generally appeals to a specific age audience. For a large majority of stations, the format is a specific type of music, but some stations find that all-news and all-talk formats also attract large audiences, especially among older listeners.

Radios, both AM and FM, have a special niche in the automobile, where they are listened to by Americans on the go. Portable radios also accompany people to the beach, to mountain resorts, to the classroom, to parties. They make and break recording artists and make and break the current events of the hour.

Economically, radio stations are holding their own. The dollar has not deserted radio. In fact, advertising revenues have soared to well above the postwar figures. But costs have risen, as have the number of stations, so the advertising butter must be spread thinly.

Television

The first experiments with television employed a *mechanical scanning* process originally invented by German Paul Nipkow in 1884. This process was dependent on a wheel that contained tiny holes positioned spirally. Behind the wheel was placed a small picture. As the wheel turned, each hole scanned one line of the picture.

Even though this device could scan only very small pictures, attempts were made to promote it commercially. C. F. Jenkins, an American, developed a workable system and formed a company in 1930 to exploit the idea. John Baird of Britain obtained a television license in 1926 and convinced the British Broadcasting Corporation to begin experimental broadcasting with a mechanical system.

At General Electric's plant in Schenectady, New York, Ernst F. W. Alexanderson began experimental programming in the 1920s using a revolving scanning wheel and an image that was 3" x 4". One of his programs, a science fiction thriller of a missile attack on New York, scanned an aerial photograph of New York that moved closer and closer and then disappeared to the sound of an explosion.

While mechanical scanning was being promoted, other people were developing *electronic scanning*, the system that has since been adopted. One was Allen B. Dumont, who developed the *oscilloscope,* or *cathode-ray tube (CRT)*, a basic electronic research tool that is similar to the TV receiver tube. Dumont was able to capitalize on this invention when the TV receiver market took hold in the 1940s.

Another early electronic inventor was Philo T. Farnsworth, who in 1922 astounded his Idaho high school teacher with diagrams for an electronic TV system. He convinced a backer to provide him with equipment and in 1927 transmitted still pictures and bits of film. He applied for a patent and found himself battling the giant of electronic TV development, RCA. In 1930 Farnsworth, at the age of twenty-four, won his patent and later received royalties from RCA.

In 1932 experimental broadcasts were transmitted from the Empire State Building. Three years later, in the midst of the depression, RCA announced that the company would invest millions in the further development of television.

RCA decided to have television displayed at the 1939 New York World's Fair. President Roosevelt appeared on camera and was seen on sets with five or seven-inch tubes. Other companies established experimental stations and broadcast in New York. Sets, mostly manufactured by RCA and Dumont, had increased tube sizes to twelve inches and sold for $200 to $600. CBS began

Figure 2. 5.

Television....

Show us the world in pictures!

experimentation with color television, utilizing a mechanical color wheel of red, blue, and green that transferred color to the images. This color system was not compatible with the RCA-promoted system. In other words, the sets being manufactured could not receive either color or black and white pictures from the CBS mechanical system, and proposed CBS receivers would not be able to pick up existing black and white pictures.

In 1940 a group led mainly by RCA personnel tried to convince the FCC to allow the operation of the 441-line system. However, the FCC was not certain that this system had adequate technical quality so it established an industrywide committee of engineers, the National Television System Committee (NTSC), to recommend standards. This committee rejected the 441-line system and recommended the 525-line system, which the United States presently uses. CBS approached the committee with the idea of color television, but the committee did not think the system was of sufficient quality.

In May of 1941 the FCC authorized the full operation of 525-line black and white television. Originally there were to be thirteen very high frequency (VHF) channels, but channel I was eliminated to allow spectrum space for FM radio. Twenty-three stations went on the air, 10,000 sets were sold, and commercials were sought. The first commercial was bought by Bulova for $900 and consisted of a shot of a Bulova clock with an announcer intoning the time.

Television grew so uncontrollably in 1948 that in the fall of that year the FCC imposed a freeze on television station authorizations because stations were beginning to interfere with each other.

In 1952, the FCC engineers determined that there was not adequate room left in the VHF band, and they opted for adding seventy stations in the UHF band, for a total of eighty-two channels. UHF was at a much higher frequency than VHF, and very little was known about the technical characteristics of UHF at that time. However, the FCC engineers felt that by increasing the power and tower height of UHF stations, they would be equal in coverage to VHF stations.

Instant replay became an instant hit with sports fans, and the Super Bowl telecast of 1967 was preceded by much hoopla. As remote equipment made it easier to leave the studio, the quantity of sports broadcasting increased, and sports themselves changed to accommodate the new medium. Teams changed their playing times in order to avail themselves of larger audiences and added a few more playoffs to increase the excitement.

Two experiments of the 1970s involving the government were *primetime* access and the *family hour*. Prime-time access was promoted primarily by Westinghouse Broadcasting. It pointed out that the networks monopolized prime time by programming from 7:00-9:00 P.M. and suggested that some of this time should be programmed by the stations themselves in order to meet community needs, as well as to allow more room for syndicated programs.

In 1984 FCC deregulated television. TV station licenses are now given for five years instead of three, and TV stations in small communities no longer need to keep logs or ascertain community needs. In addition, there are no restrictions governing the amount of commercial time stations can program. Ownership was also somewhat deregulated. Previously, one entity could only own seven TV stations. But as of April 1985, this number was increased to twelve, provided the twelve stations are not in markets that collectively contain more than 25 percent of the nation's TV homes.

Public Broadcasting

Through concerted effort, educators persuaded the government to reserve stations in the FM band for educational broadcasting. Most of these stations exist on modest budgets provided by educational institutions, and on endowments, grants, and public donations. They do provide a hallmark of cultural programming, including classical music and some highly rated programs from National Public Radio.

Public television began with stations specifically reserved for it, but educational institutions were unable to bear as large a percentage of the costs as they had for radio. Fortunately, the Ford Foundation underwrote much of the early development of educational TV. But it could not shoulder the entire weight, so the government, amid much controversy, began in 1962 to provide grant money for facilities only.

Still, educational broadcasting was not able to compete in the free enterprise system with its commercial counterparts. The Carnegie Commission spent several years studying the situation and recommended a public television system heavily supported by government funds for both facilities and programming. The Carnegie plan was quickly passed by Congress. By recommending that the Corporation for Public Broadcasting act as a buffer and administer funds to the Public Broadcasting Service and those producing programs, the Carnegie Commission hoped to avoid the pitfall of government influence over programming. But such was not to be, and both internal and external schisms over programming philosophy rocked the CPB-PBS-NPR family during the Nixon administration. Following that, the government withdrew much of its funding, leaving public broadcasting to find other methods of financing.

The triangle formed by democracy, free enterprise, and culture has created many controversies as public broadcasting tries to maintain an equilibrium among government influence, corporate influence, and audience demographics. Just where public broadcasting is headed is unclear. But this is nothing new for an industry an has spent most of its life in a state of uncertainty.

Cable TV

Cable TV has undergone many changes, especially in recent times. What started as one- to three-channel systems in the 1950s has gone to systems of over one hundred channels. A technology that involved only wires has now wholeheartedly embraced satellites.

An industry that maintained stable, modest, consistent numbers for decades suddenly boasted figures that jumped hundreds of percentage points in one year.

The whole regulatory scene has undergone evolution. Early cable TV was essentially unregulated with rules arising only as broadcasters convinced the federal government of the need to protect them from encroachment by the cable systems. The government's reaction, primarily from Congress and the FCC, was one of confusion and abstention, but during the 1960s and early 1970s rules were enacted dealing with "must carry," distant signal importation, syndicated exclusivity, copyright, and classes of cable channels. As the government developed a deregulation policy during the 1980s, cable TV became even less regulated by both federal and local agencies than it had been.

Cable programming became a glamour business with material distributed on both a national and local basis. A multitude of pay services and basic services emanated from the satellites, and the cable systems themselves revived the concept of local programming, often with the promise of numerous local channels to meet various needs within the community. The interactive services that had been long on talk and short on action began to undergo experimentation. In recent years, the cable TV approach to programming changed the entire face of the cable industry. The cable industry is still in a state of flux, making it an exciting phenomenon. Its future course has yet to be determined.

References

Atkin, David. (1990). How Presence of Cable Affects Parental Mediation of TV Viewing. *Journalism Quarterly*, Fall, 557-563.

Balle, Francis. (1989). The Information Society, Schools, and the Media. *(ERIC Document Reproduction Service No. ED327210).*

Blyth, John and Blyth, Mary. (1985). *Telecommunications: Concepts, Development, and Management..* Mission Hills, CA: Glencoe Publishing Company:

Eastman, Susan, Head, Sydney, and Klein, Lewis. (1985). *Broadcast/Cable Programming.* Belmont, CA: Wadsworth.

Gross, Lynne. (1986). *Telecommunications: An Introduction to Radio, Television, and Other Electronic Media.* 2nd ed. Dubuque, IA: Wm. C. Brown Publishers.

Jesperson, James and Randolph, Jane. (1980). *The Story of Telecommunications.* New York: Atheneum Publishers, Inc .

Pool, Ithiel de Sola, ed. (1977). *The Social Impact of the Telephone.* Cambridge, MA: MIT Press.

Schwager, Istar. (1991). Educational TV Goes to School. *Principal*, January, 49-50.

Chapter Three

Understanding
Telecommunications
Systems

Introduction

In this age of computers, educators often find it convenient to exchange information as well as messages—for example, to connect microcomputers to a mainframe computer or to connect microcomputers to each other and access databases or share resources. We are living in the information age. The amount of information available to us is accelerating rapidly. More books are being published and magazine and journal articles written than ever before, to say nothing of the increasing numbers of research reports and all of the information generated by computers. Learning to cope with this vast array of information is a challenge that must be continually addressed. The telecommunication systems will ensure that the right information is available and accessible when needed, but sifting and selecting the right information to meet our needs is our responsibility. Computers can be of significant help in the information screening process.

Basic Elements of a Telecommunications System

A telecommunications system contains three basic elements: *transmitter* or *source, medium,* and *destination* or *receiver.* In a classroom, for example, the instructor can be a source, the students are the destinations, and the lecture is the medium. In a telegraph system, a sending key is used to create electrical impulses which travel through the wire to a receiving key. In short, information from a source via a channel is transmitted to a receiver. If no information is present, the communication becomes *noise*. Figure 3.1 illustrates this process.

Sending forth the signals is not enough to ensure communication. There must also be some involvement or activity on the part of the receiver(s) at the destination(s) to complete the exchange of information. Communication has not occurred unless the destination can understand or interpret the signals received. Thus if an instructor lectures in French and the students understand only English, chances are extremely slim that the lesson is communicated, even though transmission takes place.

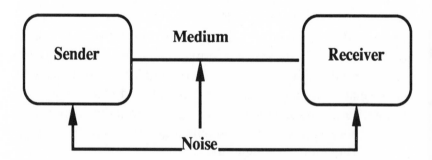

Figure 3.1. *Process of communication*

Telecommunications System

A *system* can be defined broadly as a collection of components that together accomplish a job or task. For example, a telecommunications system comprises all the components required to provide communication. The simplest system is two people talking together on the telephone. A simplified telephone system might incorporate a variety of components: telephone instruments, wires to connect the phones to the local office, a network of wires to connect various offices, account numbers, dialing conventions, billing procedures, switching mechanisms, and people who operate and maintain services. Thus the basic components of a telecommunications system are: *hardware*, *software*, *data*, *procedures*, and *personnel*. The simplified telephone system has components in each category: telephones are hardware, billing procedures are implemented in software, the items discussed during a call are data, and personnel use and maintenance of the equipment make up the specific procedures.

Hardware

Telecommunication hardware includes all of the equipment that is employed to generate, transmit, receive, and interpret the signals that represent the data to be communicated. Terminals and computers are the sources and destinations of interest. The signals that can be generated and then interpreted on receipt are not usually in a form convenient for transmission through the communication medium. Signal conversion devices are thus required to interface sources and destinations with the medium. A telephone mouthpiece is an example of an interface. A diaphragm within the mouthpiece converts the sounds from the source into electrical impulses that can be transmitted through the telephone wires. At the other end, the receiver takes the electrical impulses from the wires and uses them to drive a diaphragm to reconstruct sounds. Internally, the telephone network may encompass various media between the calling and receiving telephones, requiring intermediate interfaces for conversions that are invisible to subscribers.

Software

The software in a typical communications system can be divided into two categories: communication software actually assists the hardware in transferring the data between source and destination; management software coordinates or directs the use of communication resources in the system. Both types of software provide control functions to maximize system performance and flexibility. Additionally, software is often more easily changed in response to changes in technology or regulations.

A particularly useful tool for structuring our investigation of data communication software is the reference model for Open Systems Interconnection (OSI), developed by the International Standards Organization (ISO). This model was designed as a vendor-independent approach to describing the communication functions required to support computing. It works both as a framework for analysis of existing networks and products and as a guide for implementing new systems. In fact, the desire to conform to OSI standards has shaped the evolution of old products and the design of new products from many computer and communication vendors.

Data

There are two fundamental types of data to be communicated by the systems: *characters,* the letters, digits, and punctuation we normally think of as text; and *numbers,* the numerals and symbols used for arithmetic manipulation. Both are stored and handled internally to computers in a binary form represented by strings of ones and zeroes. Many computers use ASCII (American Standard Code for Information Interchange) to represent characters.

Large IBM computers use EBCDIC (Extended Binary Coded Decimal Interchange Code), however, and can directly handle ASCII only under special circumstances. Normally, ASCII characters must be translated into EBCDIC for processing by IBM equipment.

Procedures

Many procedures for data communication are built into the other components of a communications system. The hardware and software elements can be considered as particular ways of implementing some of the required procedures, and data formats can be considered the result of a negotiation procedure to determine the language for communication. Consequently, our discussion of procedures addresses how the hardware, software, data, and personnel interact to communicate as required by the information system application. For example, most systems have procedures for detecting service interruptions, identifying the faulty components, and isolating them for repair. These used to be accomplished manually, but many of these procedures are now being automated.

It is good practice to have written operating procedures reviewed by someone who does not usually perform them, to ensure that the procedures are explicit and complete. Our primary concern with operating procedures will be how increased automation affects system operations and what impacts new technology generates. In a telephone system, for example, consider the change from a receptionist-operated switchboard to automatic call completion in terms of any differences in interaction among subscribers and the required hardware changes.

Personnel

Outside of procedures, the personnel aspects of communication systems are not treated separately or in detail. We simply assume that the purpose of the system is to be the linking mechanism between a person or computer program as the source and some other person or program as the destination.

Transmission Channels

Transmission media carry information from one site to another. *Twisted-pair wires, coaxial cables, microwaves, satellites, laser*, and *fiber optics* are some of the widely-used media.

Twisted-Pair Wire

The medium most familiar for transmission of communication signals is probably copper wires. Over the years, telephone companies have laid millions of miles of wires into virtually every home and organization in the country. The copper wires are twisted in pairs, one wire carrying the signal and one wire completing the electrical circuit (with ground). The twisted pairs are often bundled together into multi-pair cables for convenient handling and economic packaging. Adjacent pairs must be twisted in different patterns to minimize crosstalk (signal leakage from one pair to another).

The primary advantage of twisted-pair wires is the cost. Wire is readily available from many vendors and can be installed with simple and inexpensive hand tools without a great deal of skill required.

Despite its advantages, twisted-pair wire has limitations that prevent its use in some applications. Twisted-pair wires need repeaters every one to four miles apart. These pieces of equipment are very expensive and costly to repair, thus long-term maintenance costs are high. Twisted-pair wire is susceptible to the effects of weather. Also, when security is important, twisted-pair wire is a poor choice, for it is easily tapped.

Coaxial Cable

Coaxial cable is a special wire which has the capacity to carry TV signals, voice, and data communications. It is cost effective for use at distances less than 15 miles.

A coaxial cable consists of a hollow copper cylinder or other cylindrical conductors surrounding a single copper wire conductor. An insulator occupies the space between the outer shell and the inner conductor.   A coaxial cable can transmit much higher frequencies than a twisted pair wire. A single coaxial tube carries 3600 voice channels. They can handle a bandwidth of up to 400 MHz.

The additional cost of coaxial cable is justified by the following advantages:

— A much larger number of channels can be sent over one cable
— Negligible crosstalk between channels
— Lower delay distortion
— Wide availability
— Moderate cost
— Multidrop suitability
— Ease of configurability

Coaxial cable also has some disadvantages. Like the twisted pair wire, coaxial cable is difficult to install. The cable itself is bulky and rigid. Coaxial cable is susceptible to minimal crosstalk. Security may also be a problem.   In addition, coaxial cable has high long-term maintenance costs due to the many repeaters used.

Microwave

Microwave signals travel on a straight line and have difficulty penetrating heavy rain, trees, and buildings. Microwave signals are limited to line of sight. To reach locations beyond 30 miles, a repeater is used. The repeaters receive signals, amplify them, then retransmit them to the next repeater. A repeater station can cost as much as $50,000.

Microwave radio is the medium most used by the common microwave radio transmissions which occur in the 4-28 GHz frequency range. Microwave radio transmission carries for long distances. Microwave signals may carry data in either analog or digital form. Voice, data, and television signals are carried, but each is given its own channel. Depending on the transmission frequency used, some microwave signals are subject to interference by heavy rain; therefore, when a microwave system is designed, provision must be made for this possibility.

Microwave clearly offers many advantages. Possibly the most important is that microwave transmission has the potential for carrying high traffic volumes. Ease of installation and ability to travel to places where cable placement may be impossible, such as rocky and mountainous terrain, make microwaves special in telecommunication. Microwaves are also useful in connecting LANs or for linking a LAN with distant terminals. Among the limitations are that microwave towers or repeaters must be built with a clear line of sight. Reflections from unanticipated objects, such as helicopters or new skyscrapers, may cause interference. Microwave transmission is not easily secured. It is impossible to prevent unauthorized detection of data signals over a microwave path so when security is important, encryption or scrambling is required.

Satellite

A satellite acts as a relay station in outer space. It is placed in a geosynchronous orbit 22,300 miles above the earth's surface. It receives signals from a ground station, amplifies these signals, and retransmits them to another ground station (satellite dish). Using a satellite system is very costly as one satellite can cover about 40 percent of the earth. Figure 3.2 illustrates satellite transmission.

Radiowaves can not be bent, but they can be sent over great distances in a straight line; therefore, signals can be sent from

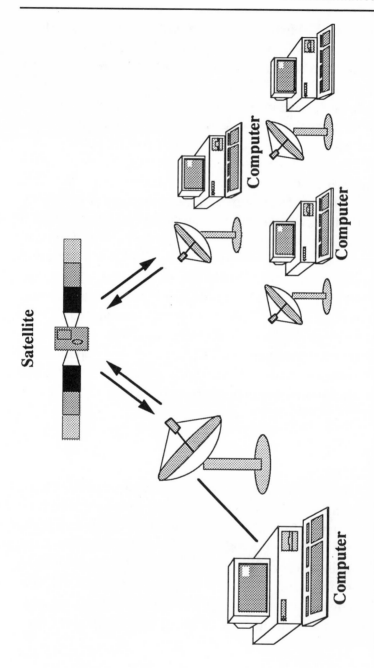

Figure 3.2. *Satellite Transmission. Data uplink 22,300 miles from the sender to the satellite and downlink 22,300 miles to the receiver.*

earth to a satellite and returned to a different location on Earth. The satellites appear to be stationary in the sky because they revolve around the earth once in 24 hours at the exact speed of Earth. Satellites are powered by solar batteries and can be left unattended and unserviced. They remain in the same position for many years aided only by firing small gas jets when occasional course corrections are necessary. Though a satellite is far enough away from the earth that its signals can cover about 40% of the earth, it may be necessary to utilize two satellites for some world wide transmissions. Satellites can be spaced 3-5 degrees apart. Any closer spacing would cause microwave beams from adjacent satellites to interfere with each other. Today most satellites have transponders with a bandwidth of 36 MHz. Like microwave links, they can handle several thousand voice circuits. Each transponder may be used to carry any of the following:

— One color television channel with sound
— 1200 voice channels
— A data rate of 50 megabytes per second (mbps)
— The center 24 MHz of each band may relax either
    16 channels of 1,54 Mbps, or
    400 channels of 64,000 bps, or
    600 channels of 40,000 bps

Each communication satellite is capable of handling 24 channels, 12 horizontal and 12 vertical. A major advantage of satellite transmission is its ability to transmit a great amount of data over a long distance which would be costly otherwise. The cost of satellite transmission is declining; likewise, the cost of Earth stations are declining too. One of the best uses of satellites is for broadcasting. It is excellent for remote areas.

Aircraft passing through the satellite beam may cause interference. Satellite transmissions can be received by anyone and care should be taken to insure a secure system. Satellite transmissions are currently used for the purpose of reaching isolated places on the earth, an alternative to suboceanic cables, long-distance domestic telephone and television links, television and music broadcasting facilities, a data facility capable of interlinking computer terminals everywhere, and a multiple-access facility capable of carrying all types of signals on a demand basis.

Fiber Optics

Optical fibers are glass-like fibers that are used to carry laser beams to far distances. It is an expensive medium, but immune to weather and unauthorized intrusion.

Optical fibers are firm, flexible glass hairs (filaments) used to transmit pulses of light created by a laser . By turning these pulses of light into a computer code, the laser can send massive amounts of information through the fiber. The laser makes use of a binary code by transmitting a pulse for a "one" and no light for a "zero."

Fiber optic bandwidth is specified as a function of distance. A 0.25-inch diameter cable containing two optical waveguides can carry the same volume of communications as a 3-inch diameter cable containing 20,000 copper wires. Experiments conducted at Bell Labs demonstrated a capacity to transmit two billion bits, or twenty five million words of text, every second, through a 7- mile piece of fiber without any amplification. Fiber optics, in addition to offering larger initial capacity, can offer a good potential for expansion to accommodate traffic growth. Some additional advantages are a larger bandwidth, low loss, small size, light weight, ease of installation, and low cost per circuit mile. In addition to the preceding advantages, fiber optic systems are resistant to intrusion and therefore can be used to secure transmission.

As with any new technology, fiber optics has its share of disadvantages. Stress, due to tension or sharp bending, makes fiber optics become fatigued and exhibit loss of strength and eventually it costs more than other media and it is complex to interconnect and not practical for low traffic application.

Laser

Laser (Light Amplification by Stimulated Emission of Radiation) is a device that creates a special beam of light that has tremendous capacity for carrying information. It has been estimated that a single laser beam could transmit all the telephone calls of the world simultaneously. Unfortunately, since a laser is basically a beam of light, fog, rain, and snow severely limit its range. The effective range is 1/2 mile for reliability. It is ideal between two buildings in crowded cities.

Modes of Transmission

There are several transmission schemes: *simplex, half duplex*, and *full duplex*.

Simplex

Simplex transmits data in one direction only. It will either send only or receive only. Radio is an example of simplex. Figure 3.3 illustrates the simplex transmission.

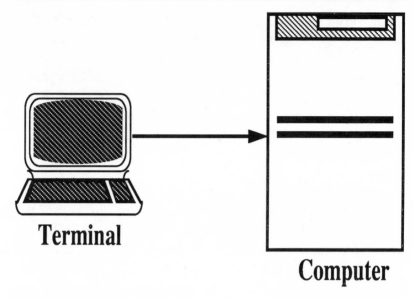

Figure 3.3. *Simplex Transmission, one-way transmission only.*

Half Duplex

Here, data transmission can be in either direction, but in only one direction at a time. CB radio is an example of half duplex. Figure 3.4 shows the half duplex transmission. In half duplex transmission mode, computers use special control signals, built into most serial interfaces, to negotiate which system will send data and which will receive data. The most commonly used control signals for this type of communication are *request to send (RTS)* and *clear to send (CTS)*. The amount of time it takes computers using half duplex communications to switch between sending and receiving is called *turnaround time*. For example, assume a message is sent from your modem to a distant modem. At completion of that message transmission, there is a certain amount of turnaround time while the modem at the receiving end changes from receive to transmit, as well as from request to send to clear to send.

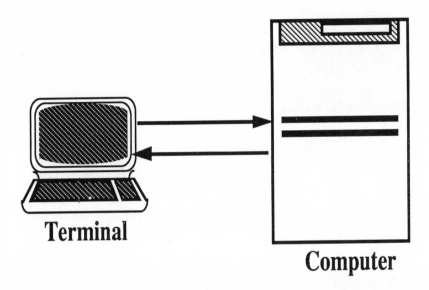

Figure 3.4. *Half-Duplex Transmission, two-way transmission, but only one-way at a time.*

Full Duplex

In full duplex, data transmissions occur in both directions simultaneously. Telephone is an example of full duplex. Full duplex requires a front-end processor that has the proper software for simultaneous two-way communication. Figure 3.5 illustrates the full duplex transmission.

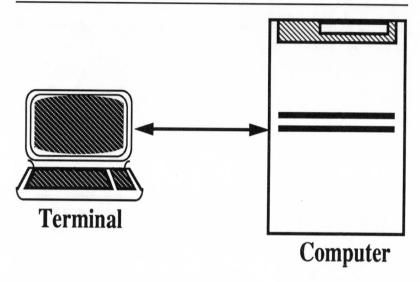

Terminal

Computer

Figure 3.5. *Full-Duplex Transmission, two-way transmission simultaneously.*

Analog and Digital Signals

If information has to be transferred from one place to another, this can be done in writing, as in a letter or newspaper, for example. Telecommunication transfers information in the form of electrical signals as a continuous cycle called *analog,* or in the form of pulses, called *digital.*

Analog signals are defined as continuous electrical signals that vary in voltage. Digital signals are described as discontinuous electrical signals that change from one state (on) to another state (off) in discrete steps. Figure 3.6 shows analog and digital signals.

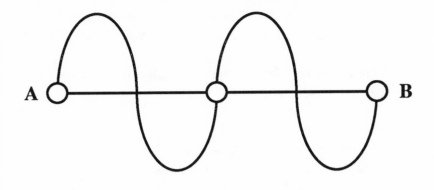

Analog Signals

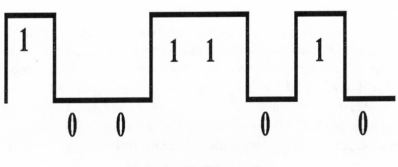

Digital Signals

Figure 3.6. *Analog and Digital Signals. A digital signal is a series of stop-start pulses. An analog signal is a series of continuous cycles.*

A *Cycle* is defined as a completed occurrence per second. If a cycle is completed in one second, it has a frequency of one cycle per second.

The number of cycles per unit of time is called *frequency* and is measured in *Hertz (Hz)*.

1 Hz = 1 cycle per second
1 KHz= 1,000 cycles per second (Kilo Hertz)
1 MHz=1,000,000 cycles per second (Mega Hertz)
1 GHz= 1,000,000,000 cycles per second (Giga Hertz)

Human speech is made up of frequencies ranging from 150 Hz to around 8 KHz. Speech transmitted at frequencies between 300 and 3,400 Hz is still intelligible. One telephone channel carrying speech has a bandwidth of about 3 KHz.

Digital signals are either in the on or off position. Either position is called a BIT. Approximately ten bits equals 1 analog. As a result, more bandwidth is necessary for a digital system to transmit the same information. For example, a 4 KHz analog signal requires 64,000 bit-per second (bps) in digital to have the same clarity, while a 4.5 MHz TV signal, for instance, requires 90 million bps (90 Mbps) to present the same analog picture and sound quality. Digital transmission has the following advantages:

— Less susceptible to interference and noise
— Can be stored and manipulated by computer
— Costs less if computer-oriented long-distance networks
   are used

Bandwidth

Bandwidth is the range of lowest and highest frequencies that are transmitted. The wider the bandwidth, the more information (video, audio, data) transmitted in a given period of time. Bandwidths, along with distance and duration of transmission, are determining factors in communication costs.

There are three categories of bandwidths: *narrowband, voiceband,* and *broadband.*

Narrowband is used for nonvoice service such as telegraph and low-speed data transmission. [0 -300 HZ, 5-30 characters per second (cps), or 40-100 baud per second (bps)]

Voiceband is used for voice and data transmission. (30 -3300 HZ, over 1000 cps, or 110-9600 bps)

Broadband is used for high-speed data and video transmission. (3300+ HZ, 100,000+ cps, or several Mbps). Video signals are transmitted on broadband since they require a wider band because of the nature of the signal and the amount of the information in a television picture. For comparison purposes, an average TV set has 300 horizontal lines and 430 light points on each line, for a total of 140,000 discrete points of light which are referred to as *picture elements.* To have a sense of motion, 30 frames move each second for total of 4,200,000 picture elements each second, which requires a bandwidth of roughly 4,500,000 Hz (4.5 MHz). The telephone company can pack over 1,000 telephone conversations into a 4.5 MHz bandwidth.

A transmission line called T1 is used to transmit at a rate of 1.544 million bits of information per second. The T1 line can carry videoconferences, phone calls, and data, concurrently. Video transmission is very expensive. However, by compressing the signals, videoconferencing is becoming more affordable. A *codec* (coder-decoder) device takes the standard analog TV signal, converts it to a digital data stream, and compresses it by up to 99%. The signals are then decoded at the receiving end. This compression enables cost-effective transmission of two-way videoconferencing.

Noise

Noise is defined as signal elements received at a destination that were not intentionally transmitted as part of (or in support of) the information being communicated. In a simple term, noise is considered as any unwanted signal in a transmission path. Noise and distortion can cause data communication errors. It is introduced by equipment or natural disturbances, and it degrades the performance of a communication line. If noise occurs, the errors are manifested as extra or missing bits.

Noise can be recognized in many forms. The familiar background "hiss" or static on radio and telephones is known as *white noise*. It is caused by the thermal agitation of electrons and therefore is inescapable. Even if the equipment were perfect and the wires were perfectly insulated from any and all external interference, there would still be some noise. This kind of noise usually is not a problem unless its level becomes so high that it obliterates the data transmission. Sometimes noise from other sources such as power line induction, cross modulation from adjacent lines, and a conglomeration of random signals induces white noise even though it is not caused by thermal electrons.

Impulse noise, or *spikes,* is the primary source of errors in data communications. An impulse of noise can last as long as 1/100th of a second. An impulse of this duration is heard as a click or a crackling noise during voice communications. This click does not affect voice communications, but it might obliterate a group of data bits, causing a burst error on a data communication line. At

150 bits per second, 1 or 2 bits would be changed by a spike of 1/100th of a second, whereas at 4800 bits per second, 48 bits would be changed. Some of the sources of impulse noise are voltage changes in adjacent lines or circuitry surrounding the data communication line.

Amplitude noise involves a sudden change in the level of power. The effect of this noise depends on the type of modulation being used by the modem. Some of the causes of amplitude noise may be faulty amplifiers, dirty contacts with variable resistances, sudden added loads by new circuits being switched on during the day, maintenance work in progress, and switching to different transmission lines.

Line outages are a catastrophic cause of errors and incomplete transmission. Occasionally, a communication circuit fails for a brief period of time. This type of failure may be caused by faulty telephone equipment.

Echo

Data travel either on a two-wire circuit, where there are only two wires from modem to modem, or on a four-wire circuit, where there are four wires from modem to modem. Two-wire circuits have a problem of echoes. When people talk on a two-wire circuit, echoes may occur under some conditions. Echoes arise in telephone circuits for the same reason that acoustic echoes occur; there is a reflection of the electrical waves from the far end of the circuit. The telephone company provides echo suppression circuits to stop echoes during voice conversation. An echo suppressor permits transmission in only one fixed direction. These echo suppressors open and close on two-wire lines during data transmissions.

References

Birnie, Wendy. (1989). Networking into the Nineties. *Accountancy,* September, 32-33.

Blegen, August. (1990). Opportunity for Network Advances. *Communications News,* March, 51.

Blyth, John and Blyth, Mary. (1985). *Telecommunications: Concepts, Development, and Management.* Mission Hills, CA: Glencoe Publishing Company .

Clancy, David. (1989). Electronic Communication More Than a Fashion Fad. *Transmission and Distribution,* October, 46+.

DeNoia, Lynn A. (1987). Data Communication Fundamentals and Applications. Columbus, OH: Merrill Publishing Co.

Edwards, Morris. (1988). International Data Services: Satellites, Fiber Optics Help Create Global Village. *Communications News,* December, 45-49.

Finneran, Michael. (1990). *Business Communications Review,* February, 78-80+.

Green, James Harry. (1986). *The Dow Jones-Irwin Handbook of Telecommunications.* Homewood, IL: Dow Jones-Irwin.

Herrmann, F. et al. (1985). Information and Its Carriers. *Physics Education,* September, 206-210.

Jander, Mary and Strauss, Paul. (1990). Affordable Fax/ Data Gear on Way. *Communications News,* March, 43-45.

Koenig, Michael. (1984). Fiber Optics and Library Technology. *Library Hi Tech,* January, 9-15.

McGroger, Alice. (1989). Communication: Key to Success. *Business Credit,* July-August, 3+.

Chapter Four

Data Communications Systems

Introduction

The increasing use of computers in educational operations has created the need for rapid movement of data from one location to another. In its broadest sense, data can be communicated by physical transportation—messengers, trucks, or airplanes—or by electrical means—input and output devices, electrical transmission links, and associated switching equipment. In many cases, the best way to get information from one place to another is by mail; this method is usually the most economical. However, when rapid transmission of information is important, electronic methods are required.

One of the first business applications of data communications was the Sabre airline reservation system, developed jointly by IBM and American Airlines. After six years of development, the system began operation in 1962. Business and educational organizations are increasingly recognizing the advantages of data networks. Although only about one percent of the computers sold in 1965 were linked to a data communication system, virtually all computers sold or leased in the United States today have communications capabilities.

Definition of Data Communications

Data communications is the movement of encoded information from one point to another by means of electrical or optical transmission systems. Such systems often are called *data communication networks*. In general, these networks are established to collect data from remote points (usually terminals or microcomputers) and transmit that data to a central point equipped with a computer or another terminal, or to perform the reverse process, or some combination of the two. Data communication networks facilitate more efficient use of central computers. They improve the day-to-day control of a business by providing faster information flow. They provide message switching services to allow terminals to talk to one another. In general, they offer better and more timely interchange of data among their users and bring the power of computers closer to more users.

The objectives of most data communication networks are to

— Reduce the time and effort required to perform various tasks
— Capture data at its source
— Centralize control over data
— Effect rapid dissemination of information
— Reduce current and future costs
— Support expansion of organization at reasonable incremental cost as the organization grows
— Support organizational objectives in centralizing or decentralizing computer systems
— Support improved management control of the organization

While data communications might be used in many different situations, educational operations that exhibit some of the following characteristics usually can benefit from the use of a data communications network.

— Widespread use of microcomputers
— Decentralized operations
— A high volume of educational software, organizational mail, messenger service, or telephone calls between the various schools (the voice communication corridors, that is, telephone calls, may become or be replaced by the data transfer corridors)
— Repetitive paperwork operations, such as the recreation or copying of information
— Inefficient and time-consuming retrieval of information
— Inadequate control of the educational information
— Inadequate educational planning and forecasting

Basic Components of a Communication System

Like any other communication system, a data communication system consists of the source, the medium, and the receiver (see chapter three). The source is the originator of the information; the medium is the path through which the information flows; and the receiver is the mechanism that accepts the information. In this definition, a terminal or microcomputer often alternates as both a source and a receiver. The medium is nothing more than the communication line (or circuit) over which the information travels. Usually, the lines are leased from a "common carrier" such as the Bell Operating Companies, AT&T, MCI, or US SPRINT, although an organization can install its own lines. A *common carrier* is a company recognized by the Federal Communications Commission (FCC) or an appropriate state licensing agency as having the right to furnish communication services to individual subscribers, schools, or business organizations.

Telecommunications and teleprocessing are other terms used to describe data transmission between a computing system and remotely located devices. The terms data communications, telecommunications, and teleprocessing are used interchangeably by many writers in this field.

A sender is usually a terminal. It also might be a microcomputer, a video terminal, or some other type. Once the user has entered a message, it goes to the encoder, which usually is called the *modem*. The modem coverts the signal from its direct electrical pulses (baseband) into a series of varying frequency tones (broadband). The purpose of this encoding process is to put the transmission into a mode that is compatible with the various transmission media such as twisted-pair wire, microwave, satellite, fiber optic, or other facilities.

These transmission media are referred to as a *circuit*. These are the telephone company circuits over which the message moves. Finally, when the message reaches the distant host computer, it passes through the decoder, which is another modem, then reaches the host computer.

Figurer 4.1 depicts a basic data communication system. This system includes terminals, connector cables, a line-sharing device, modems, local loops, telephone company switching offices, interexchange channel (IXC) facilities, a front-end communication processor, and a host computer.

The *terminals* or *microcomputers* involve a human-to-machine interface device where people can enter and receive data or information. This type of device might have a video screen, a printing mechanism, and a keyboard. In the future this device may be voice actuated.

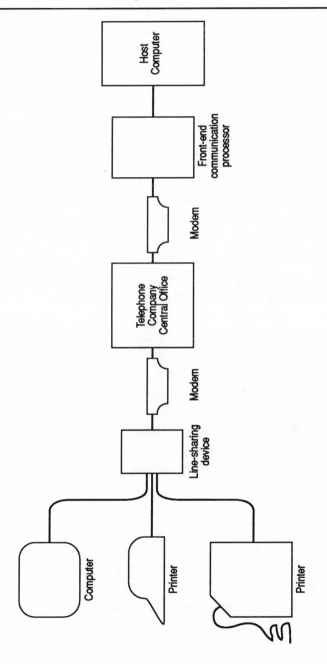

Figure 4.1. *Basic data communication system*

The *modem* is a solid state electronic device that converts direct electrical signals to modulated signals that can be sent over data communication circuits.

The *connector cables* are special cables containing many wires that interconnect the terminal to the modem.

The *line-sharing device* allows multiple terminals to share a single modem. Each terminal sequentially has its turn to transmit and receive data/information.

The *local loops* are the connections or "last mile" that interconnects schools or districts, for example, to the telephone company central office (switching office), or to the special common carrier network, if using a connection other than the telephone company.

The *central office* (sometimes called *end office* or *exchange office*) contains the various switching and control facilities that are operated by the telephone company or other special common carrier. When dial-up communication circuits are used, the data transmission goes through these switching facilities. When a private leased circuit is employed, however, the telephone company wires the circuit path around the switching facilities to provide a clear unbroken path from one modem to the other.

The *interexchange channels/circuits* (sometimes called IXC circuits) are the circuits that go from one telephone company central office to another central office. These circuits can be microwave circuits, but they also may be copper wire pairs, coaxial cables, satellite circuits, optical fibers, or other transmission medium.

The *front-end communication processor* is a specialized minicomputer with very special software programs. These software programs, along with the front-end hardware, control the entire data communication network. For example, a powerful front-end communication processor may have 100 or more modems attached to it through its ports (circuit connect points).

Finally, the *host computer* is the central processing unit (CPU) that processes requests, performs database lookups, and carries out the data-processing activities required for the educational organization.

Coding System

Many different codes are used in telecommunications systems. One of the earliest was the original Baudot code invented by Emil Baudot, a Frenchman. His work produced a code structure that was eventually standardized as CCITT (Consultative Committee on International Telegraphy and Telephony), but that code is not in use today. The name Baudot code has remained however, and it is commonly but incorrectly applied to a code that was developed by Donald Murray. The Murray code was standardized as CCITT and it is still in use.

Baudot Code

The Baudot code uses 5 bits to represent a character and has no parity bit. With 5 bits, there are 32 unique code points which are not enough to represent the alphabet, numerals, and punctuation marks. The escape mechanism used in the Baudot code is to assign two characters a unique function called the letters shift and figures shift. When a figures shift character is sent, all of the characters that follow it are treated as uppercase characters until a letters shift character is sent. Similarly, all of the characters following a letters shift are treated as lowercase characters until a figures be assigned. Since some characters must be recognized in either shift the Baudot code actually has only 58 unique characters.

The Baudot code was originally developed for the French telegraph service and is still used today in telegraph, teletypewriter, and telex communications.

A character is a symbol that has a common, constant meaning for some group of people. A character might be the letter A or B, or it might be a number such as 1 or 2. Characters may also be special symbols such as & or ?. Characters in data communications, as in computer systems, are represented by groups of bits. The various groups of bits that represent the set of characters that are the "alphabet" of any given system are called a coding system, or simply a code. This section will discuss some of the codes used in data communications.

A byte is a group of consecutive bits that are treated as a unit or character. One byte normally is comprised of 8 bits and usually represents one character. However, in data communications some codes in regular use utilize 5, 6, 7, 8, or 9 bits to represent a character. These differences in the number of bits per character arise because the codes have different numbers of characters to represent and different provisions for error checking. *Coding* is the representation of one set of symbols by another set of symbols. For example, representation of the character A by a group of 7 bits (say, 1000001) is an example of coding. As we have seen, information in data communications is normally transmitted serially over a transmission line or channel. Codes for representing the information vary both in the number of bits used to define a single character and in the assignment of bit patterns to each particular character. For example, the bit group 1000001 may represent the character A in one coding scheme (ASCII), but the bit group 11000 may represent the character A in some other code configuration.

The American Standard Code for Information Interchange (ASCII)

The American Standard Code for Information Interchange (ASCII) grew out of work done by the American National Standards Institute (ANSI) and is the most widely used code in computers and telecommunications networks today. It is the basic standard code and is available on most terminals. ASCII is a 7-bit code and therefore has 2^7 or 128 unique code points. The ASCII code for the capital letter P is 1010000 and the code for the lowercase letter s is 1110011. An extended version of ASCII adds an 8th bit. The eighth bit is the parity bit for error checking on individual characters. Parity is discussed later in this chapter.

The ASCII code is used widely on both asynchronous and synchronous data communication equipment.

Extended Binary Coded Decimal Interchange Code (EBCDIC)

EBCDIC is IBM's standard information code. This code has 256 valid character combinations because there are 8 information bits and parity is carried as a ninth bit. The 9-channel tape drive was developed originally to hold the IBM code with its 8 data bits and 1 parity bit.

It should be noted that the bit positional numbering system is different in EBCDIC and ASCII. ASCII numbers its bit positions from 8 to 1 (left to right), while EBCDIC numbers its bit positions from 0 to 7 (also left to right). In fact, IBM addresses everything left to right, such as memory, records, and bits in a byte. Figure 4.2 depicts the positional numbering system differences between EBCDIC and ASCII.

Figure 4.2. ASCII and EBCDIC Codes

Char.	ASCII	EBCDIC
====	======	======
A	01000001	11000001
B	01000010	11000010
C	01000011	11000011
D	01000100	11000100
E	01000101	11000101
F	01000110	11000110
G	01000111	11000111
H	01001000	11001000
I	01001001	11001001
J	01001010	11010001
K	01001011	11010010
L	01001100	11010011
M	01001101	11010100
N	01001110	11010101
O	01001111	11010110
P	01010000	11010111
Q	01010001	11011000
R	01010010	11011001
S	01010011	11100010
T	01010100	11100011
U	01010101	11100100
V	01010110	11100101
W	01010111	11100110
X	01011000	11100111
Y	01011001	11101000
Z	01011010	11101001
0	00110000	11110000
1	00110001	11110001
2	00110010	11110010
3	00110011	11110011
4	00110100	11110100
5	00110101	11110101
6	00110110	11110110
7	00110111	11110111
8	00111000	11111000
9	00111001	11111001

ASCII: American Standard Code for Information Interchange
EBCDIC: Extended Binary Coded Decimal Interchange Code

Code Conversion

In most data communication systems, code conversion occurs from one coding system to another. Even though ASCII is the most widely used communication code, it is not universal. Although nearly all personal computers use ASCII for both internal and communications purposes, most large IBM data processing equipment stores data in EBCDIC. Probably the most common conversion today is from ASCII to EBCDIC and back, which must be done whenever personal computers, which operate in ASCII, are connected to mainframe computers, which operate in EBCDIC.

Data must be converted twice: from ASCII to EBCDIC when it arrives at the mainframe and from EBCDIC to ASCII when it is sent to the personal computer. Code conversion is conceptually quite simple and the type of task that a computer can perform readily. Usually a table containing the target codes is stored in the memory of the computer. The binary value of the incoming character is used as an index into the table, and the target character is picked up. The process gets complicated when one code is converted to another code that uses a smaller number of bits. For example, when EBCDIC, with 256 unique characters, is converted to ASCII, with only 128 characters, many characters cannot be converted.

Data Compaction/Compression

Compaction or compression is the process of eliminating redundant characters before transmitting to save storage space or to save transmission time so the message arrives faster and costs less to send. The result is an apparent increase in transmission throughput.

Simple compacting devices scan the data stream looking for repetitive data characters and replace them with a control character, a number, and the data character. Thus, the sequence SSSSSSSSSS would become: control character, 10, S. This is a shorthand notation that says that the letter S is to be repeated 10 times. This shorthand reduces the original 10 characters to 4, which is only 40 percent of the original number of characters. This amount of reduction is typical of compaction techniques, and the process results in a substantial savings in transmission time and potentially in transmission cost.

Language always contains a great deal of repetition. Another method of compacting the data is to substitute a symbol or control character for a word that is used frequently in the text. For example, if a file of names and addresses was being transmitted and many of the addresses contained the same city name, many characters and much transmission time could be saved by substituting a one- or two-character sequence for the city name every time it appeared in the file. The shortened form would be transmitted and at the receiving end the special character sequence would be replaced by the original word. Often many blank characters are inserted in the data stream to format the output screen so an operator can read it easily. Compaction reduces the number of blanks that have to be transmitted, saves transmission time, and provides better response time to the user.

Encryption

Another reason for manipulating the data stream before transmission is to encrypt the data to keep it private or secret. For many years encryption was rarely used except by the government, but it is now gaining wider use in industry as the concern for data security grows. Financial institutions are also big users of encryption techniques to conceal account numbers and amounts in the data they transmit.

Encryption is the transformation of the data from the meaningful code that is normally transmitted to a meaningless sequence of digits and letters that must be decrypted before it becomes meaningful again. Simple encryption schemes use character substitutions. For example, an X may be substituted for a Y, a G for a B, and so forth. Unfortunately, human analysts and computers can rapidly break this type of code. Therefore, more sophisticated techniques, which take advantage of the fact that machine codes are binary digits and can be manipulated mathematically, are used. The mathematical manipulation of bits is especially feasible when computers can be used to do the transformation.

Encryption is of particular interest in data communication because of the relative vulnerability of transmission over telephone lines. The environment is different from the computer room where data is transferred over cables that run a short distance and are often heavily shielded. Data transmitted using communication lines travels relatively long distances on various media and is essentially unprotected. Voice and data transmission are both subject to tapping or other unauthorized reception.

Modern encryption techniques use a set of mathematical rules called an *algorithm* and a key that is provided by the user. The encryption algorithm may be in the public domain, but the encrypted data will still be private because of the key. The most widely used algorithm in the United States is the *data encryption standard (DES)* algorithm developed in the mid-1970s by IBM and the federal government and adopted by the National Bureau of Standards. The DES algorithm is approved by the government for encrypting unclassified data. Classified data is encrypted using sophisticated techniques developed by the CIA, the National Security Agency, and other government organizations. Naturally the details of encryption techniques for classified data are well-kept secrets.

The DES algorithm encrypts blocks of 64 bits using a 64-bit key. The output of the algorithm is a string of random bits that are transmitted. At the receiving end, the reverse process, *decryption,* occurs, using the same 64-bit key. Since the receiving end must know which key the transmitting end used, methods must be put in place to get the key from the transmitting end of the line to the receiving end and protect its confidentiality. This takes a combination of technical and management techniques.

Encryption and decryption can be performed by hardware or software. The trade-off is that hardware is faster, but software is more flexible and easier to change. Hardware circuit chips that implement the DES algorithm are available and can be put into computers or terminals to implement a hardware solution. Software is also available to perform the encryption function. Its speed is acceptable in applications when only moderate amounts of data have to be encrypted.

In the voice world, we can identify a person we are talking to by the sound of his or her voice. In most situations this is adequate. Voice encryption devices, commonly called *scramblers,* are available for voice transmissions. They make the voice transmission unintelligible to anyone without a descrambler, effectively rendering wire tapping useless. Scramblers are mostly used in the government and defense department.

The decision to encrypt data must be made carefully. The cost of the encryption hardware or software can be easily determined. The time that it takes a computer to encrypt or decrypt the data if software is used can be calculated and a monetary value placed on it. One must also calculate the throughput delays that occur during the encryption/decryption process and determine whether they are significant. Finally, the administrative or management costs of managing the keys, keeping them secure, and changing them regularly must be considered.

Modem

The processed data in a computer is formatted as digital signals. Telephone lines are designed to transmit analog signals. In order to transmit data from one computer to another over a telephone line, the digital signal must be converted to an analog signal before it is transmitted. After transmission over a telephone line, the signal must be reconverted back to a digital signal so that it can be used by the receiving computer. The process of converting a digital signal to an analog signal is called modulation. On the other hand, demodulation is the process of converting the analog signal back to a digital signal. The device that performs the conversion and reconversion is called a modem, short for modulator-demodulator. Figure 4.3 illustrates the personal computer-to-modem connection.

Modem transmission speed (modulation or demodulation) is measured in baud rate. Baud rate is the amount of time required to transmit one bit of data. Baud is often equated with bits per second (bps); however, a signal does not always carry one bit.

Data is transmitted at different speeds. Typical data transmission speeds are 300, 1200, 2400, 4800, and 9600 bps. Modems used with microcomputers typically use 300, 1200, or 2400 bps. Larger computers use 4800 or 9600 bps modem.

Modems are widely used in educational environments, especially for library research, connecting to an electronic bulletin board, sending electronic mail, connecting to other networks, connecting to supercomputers, computer conferencing, and uploading and downloading information and public domain software from database vendors such as CompuServe and the Source.

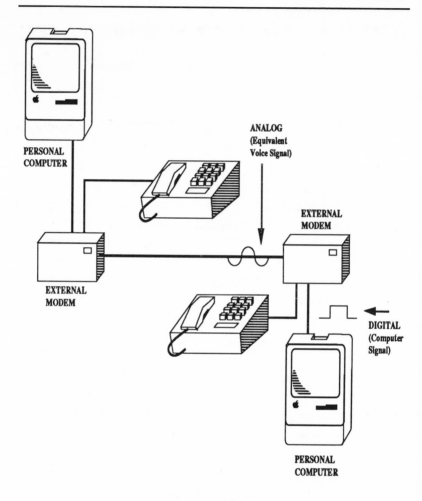

Figure 4. 3. *Modem converts digital signals from computers to analog signals that are carried over telephone lines to another modem. The receiving modem converts analog signals back into digital signals for use by computers.*

Optical Modems

This type of modem converts the electrical signals from a terminal or microcomputer to pulses of light that are transmitted down the optical fiber. Optical modems connect to RS232 and RS449 connector cables. They operate using asynchronous or synchronous transmission up to 10 million bits per second. Current models can transmit up to 5 kilometers (1 kilometer is equal to 3,280.8 feet) without using amplifiers/repeaters, but that certainly will be increased in the future, as will the 10 million bits per second speed. Within the optical modem is a laser or light-emitting diode that originates the light pulses, along with the electronics needed to convert the electrical signal prior to transmitting the digital pulses of light. A light-emitting diode transmits the data over fiber optic cable to the remote modem, which reconverts the light signal to electronic signals.

Short Haul Modems

Another type of modem is a short haul modem in which wire pair cable is used to transmit direct electrical baseband signals. Typically, these systems transmit at 19,200 bits per second over a distance of several miles. This type of modem also is called a *line driver*.

Short haul modems are used within buildings, a plant, college campus, or university facility. An example of a line driver is one that operates asynchronously over full duplex, four-wire circuits at speeds up to 19,200 bits per second for a distance of more than 1 mile. When this same line driver is used at lower speeds, transmission distance increases to 18 miles at 110 bits per second.

Schools often need short haul modems. For example, if you want to connect two classrooms together and they are several thousand feet apart, a small short haul modem may be the answer.

Acoustic Couplers

An older type of modem is an acoustic coupler. This modem is used primarily for dial-up because it can interface with any basic telephone handset. All you do is call the computer and place the telephone handset into the acoustic coupler. The coupler performs the typical modem functions of converting direct electrical signals from the terminal to frequency modulated tones (frequency shift keying) that can be sent over any telephone communication circuit.

Null Modem Cables

A null modem cable allows transmission between two microcomputers that are next to one another (within 6 to 8 feet) without the use of a modem. This specially configured cable connects the two microcomputers. The null modem cable is appropriate for connecting microcomputers in classroom.

Dumb Modems

Modems typically have been differentiated as either smart or dumb. This differentiation is based on their varying abilities to respond to a command language through which a user's communication software package instructs the modem to perform various tasks, such as dialing calls, answering incoming calls, and redialing calls. Dumb modems must be set manually for parameters of speed, originate or answer mode, and so forth. Switches are used to set these parameters, and then the user dials the call by using a telephone.

Smart Modems

By contrast, smart modems are commanded to perform their functions through the use of a command syntax language. This language is used to control their functions, such as changing speed and dialing calls. For example, if a Hayes modem is used with your microcomputer, then you might type the letters AT. These letters instruct the modem to pay attention to the next set of letters because they constitute a command or parameter change. Therefore, typing the sequence ATD tells the modem to pay attention, and the D tells it to dial a number. The complete command might be ATD555-1212, which tells the modem to pay attention, to dial a number, and to dial 555-1212.

Beyond smart modems is a classification that might be called *intelligent or advanced modem features.* These more expensive modems contain microprocessor chips and internal read only memory (ROM) coding to provide sophisticated communication protocols and diagnostic checking that run within the modem itself. For example, some modems not only perform digital-to-analog conversion but also operate as multiplexers, security restricter devices, encryption devices, error detection and retransmission devices, and so forth.

Digital Modems

If the communication circuits use digital transmission for their entire length, instead of converting to analog transmission as is done with normal telephone circuits, you have the equivalent of a digital modem. This modem shapes the digital pulses and performs all auxiliary functions needed, such as loopback testing and checking the circuit diagnostics. Its special function is to convert a digital signal to a more precise and more accurate digital signal. For example, a digital modem can take a weak electrical signal, put very precise timing characteristics between the pulses, put it out at a certain strength, and control its electrical characteristics. This is done to reduce noise, distortion, and errors. Digital modems are much simpler than digital-to-analog modems, as evidenced by their cost.

Parallel and Serial Transmission Modes

Binary data can be sent over communication circuits in either parallel or serial modes.

A parallel mode describes the way the terminal transfer of binary data is performed within a computer. In other words, if the internal structure of the computer uses an eight-bit element, then all eight bits of the element are transferred within the same computer cycle.

The same is true of the more powerful computers that use a 32-bit element or word length: all 32 bits are transferred in the same computer cycle. Parallel mode is faster and more expensive than serial mode. Figure 4.4 shows a parallel transmission mode.

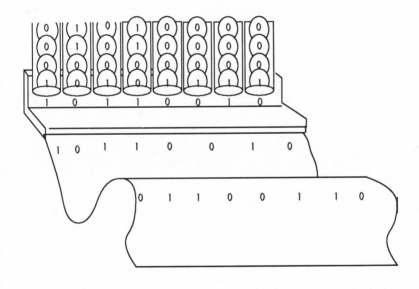

Figure 4.4. *Under parallel transmission, a series of circuits is used to transmit an entire byte at a time.*

A serial mode is used predominantly for the transfer of information in data communication. Serial transmission implies that a stream of data is sent over a communication circuit in a bit-by-bit fashion. The most common serial interface found on microcomputers is called the RS 232C. Normally with parallel transmission, several bits of a character are sent in one time cycle, whereas with serial transmission the same number of bits of a character require certain time cycles. Thus, most data communications are performed by serial transmission. Figure 4.5 illustrates a serial transmission mode.

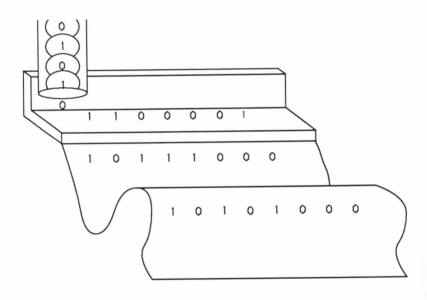

Figure 4.5. *Under serial transmission, data items are handled as a single bit stream.*

Synchronization

The process of determining and maintaining the correct timing for transmitting and receiving data is called *synchronization*. Two types of synchronization are popular: *synchronous* and *asynchronous*.

In synchronous transmission blocks of characters are sent in a continuous stream without framing bits between characters. In synchronous transmission whole blocks of data are transmitted in units. Synchronous transmission requires high data-transfer speed and is used in direct computer-to-computer communication for large computer systems.

Asynchronous transmission of data is a method in which one character is sent at a time. The transfer of data is controlled by start bits and stop bits. Because additional start and stop bits are transmitted with each character to identify the beginning and end of the group of data, each character is sent as an independent entity with start and stop bits to signal the receiver. It is used in low-speed transmitting speed, narrowband.

Synchronous transmission is much faster than asynchronous transmission and uses the faster voiceband and broadband channels but is more expensive than asynchronous transmission. Figure 4.6 illustrates synchronous and asynchronous transmission.

Line Configurations

The physical connection line between two points is referred to as a *link*. A *node* is a point of junction of the links in a network. There are two major line configurations: *point-to-point* lines and *multipoint* lines.

Point-to-point line is a direct line between a terminal and a computer system. Each terminal transmits data to and receives data from a computer system by means of an individual line that links the terminal directly to the computer system. Only one terminal is used for each line into the computer system.

Multidrop or multipoint line has more than one terminal on a single line connected to a computer system. When multidrop is used only one of the terminals at a time can transmit data at the same time. More than one terminal, however, can receive data at the same time. Figure 4.7 depicts the line configurations.

Multiplexers

Multiplexing is a process of combining the transmission, character by character, from several devices into a single communication channel. A multiplexer is required to produce multiplexing. Multiplexing transmits much more data at any one time than a single device can send.

To multiplex is to place two or more simultaneous transmissions on a single communication circuit. An important aspect of multiplexing is transparency. Transparent means that the multiplexer system does not in any way interrupt the flow of data. Neither the computer, nor the modem, nor the terminal/microcomputer using the modem knows that the multiplexer system is being used regardless of whether leased or dial-up circuits are being used. When the line is multiplexed at one end and demultiplexed at the other, each user's terminal thinks it has its own connection to the host mainframe computer. Multiplexing usually is done in multiples of 4, 8, 16, and 32 simultaneous transmissions over a single communication circuit. Multiplexers can be separated into major categories, such as frequency division multiplexers, time division multiplexers, and statistical time division multiplexers.

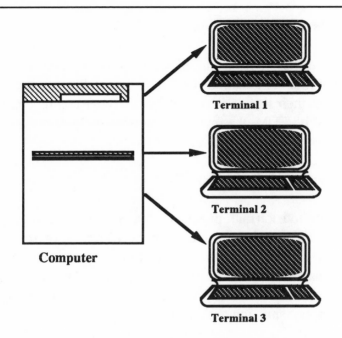

Point-to-Point Configuration

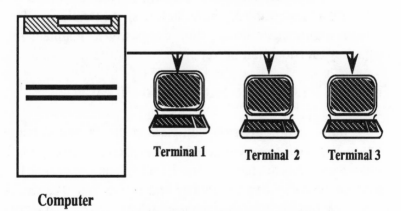

Multidrop Configuration

Figure 4. 7. *Line configurations*

Frequency Division Multiplexing (FDM)

Frequency division multiplexing can be described as having a stack of four or more modems that operate at different frequencies so that their signals can travel down a single communication circuit. With FDM, the frequency division multiplexer and the modem usually are a single piece of hardware.

Time Division Multiplexing (TDM)

Time division multiplexing is really a type of time slicing or sharing of the use of a communication circuit among two or more terminals. Each terminal takes its turn. In TDM, the multiplexer takes a character from each transmitting terminal and puts them together into a frame. The frames are put onto a high speed data stream for transmission to the other end of the circuit.

Time division multiplexing generally is more efficient than frequency division multiplexing, but it does require a separate modem. It is not uncommon to have time division multiplexers that share a line among 32 different low speed terminals. Time division multiplexers usually are less costly to maintain than frequency division multiplexers.

Statistical Time Division Multiplexing (STDM)

Statistical time division multiplexing allows the connection of more terminals to the circuit than the capacity of the circuit. In its simplest context, if there are 12 terminals connected to a statistical time division multiplexer and each terminal can transmit at 1200 bits per second, then the total is 14,400 bits per second transmitted in a given instant of time. However, if the STDM/modem/circuit combination has a maximum speed of only 9600 bits per second, then there might be a period of time when the system is loaded above its capacity.

STDM takes advantage of the fact that individual terminals are frequently idle and allows more terminals to share a line of given capacity. Students who are writing and debugging programs on a university timesharing system normally fit this model nicely.

While STDM may be very efficient, users should be aware that it can cause time delays. When traffic is particularly heavy, a user can have anywhere from a 0- to 30-second delay of data. Some data is held back by buffers when too many terminals transmit at maximum capacity for too long a period of time.

Fiber Optic Multiplexing

Fiber optic multiplexers are available, and they interconnect with the RS232, RS449, V.35, and T-1 interfaces. For example, a fiber optic multiplexer box might take up to 16 channels of data, with each channel transmitting at a capacity of 64,000 bits per channel, and multiplex it onto a 14 million bits per second fiber optic link. Fiber optic multiplexers operate similarly to time division multiplexers, but with much higher data transmission capacities. The transmission distances usually are limited to 1 to 3 miles unless amplifiers are used somewhere along the fiber optic cable.

T-1 Multiplexing

T-1 multiplexing involves a special kind of multiplexer combined with a high capacity digital service unit (DSU) made especially for managing the ends of the T-1 link. T-1 multiplexers are expensive and typically are sold based on the "port" capacity or the maximum number of devices that can be connected to the T-1 multiplexer. Because T-1 links can carry digitized voice, data, and image (video) signals, it is important to differentiate T-1 multiplexers by their ability to provide each of these three services.

One typical T-1 multiplexer can take a T-1 communication circuit that operates at 1.544 million bits per second and multiplex it onto 48 voice and data communication circuits. These 48 communication circuits can operate in either synchronous or asynchronous mode. Another T-1 multiplexer can subdivide the 1.544 million bits per second channel into 96 circuits at 9600 bits per second or even 200 channels that support 4800 bits per second. Other T-1 multiplexers can accept very high speeds (up to 768,000 bits per second for compressed video transmission) and, at the same time, multiplex lower speed (such as 4800 bits per second) data transmission paths through the multiplexer.

AT&T offers a digital multiplexer that can combine up to 28 T-1 communication channels into a single 45 million bits per second T-3 transmission facility.

Concentration is used when more devices are connected to a computer than the communication channel can handle at once. When the number of transmissions exceeds the capacity of the communication channel, the data is stored in a *buffer* for later transmission. Many multiplexers also provide concentration.

Parity Checking

A basic problem in using voice facilities for data transmission is the presence of noise and distortion which causes errors. To detect the transmission errors, parity checking technique is used. The parity checking technique is a process of adding *parity bit* to the transmitted data for detecting errors.

ASCII uses an eight-bit code, but the last code, the parity bit, is used to check a stream of ASCII characters for correct transmission from one place to another.

The parity bit is added so that the total number of 1 bits in the character will be an even (or in some cases, odd) number. If the representation for the character R is 1010010, the number of 1 bits is 3, which is an odd number, a parity bit of 1 would be added to the character so that its complete representation would be 10100101. If the representation for the letter S is 1010011, the number of 1 bits is already an even number. With an even parity system, a bit of 0 would be added, given the complete representation of **10100110.**

When the character representation is transmitted on a communication lines, and transmitter and receiver have agreed to use even parity, the receiving machine detects for an even number of 1 bits. If not, the machine detects the error.

Private Branch Exchange (PBX)

Private Automatic Branch Exchange (PBX), or computer Branch Exchange (CBX) are interchangeably used. In a single term, a private branch exchange (PBX) is an electronic switch board which routes voice and data. Because the PBX is digital moderns are needed only to access telephone lines outside the office, so the digital PBX can function as a LAN as well as a voice telephone network. The PBX is known now as an integrator of the automated office. The driving force behind the integration of data and voice in the PBX is the proliferation of terminals needed in the automated office. In the automated office the telephone will be supplemented by a data terminal for sending and receiving messages, filing and retrieving data, creating and editing text, and supporting the office workers' productivity with computer aids such as schedules, calendars, spreadsheets, and a multiplicity of other specialized tools. Some of the major features of a PBX may be as follows:

— Automatic redial
— Call forwarding
— Call transfer
— Call waiting
— Conference calls
— Speed dialing
— Data communication
— Voice messaging

A special category of PBX is the Data PBX. Data PBX are switches especially designed for switching data; they do not handle telephone calls. They connect many terminals to many computers on an as-needed basis.

A user at a terminal dials or has a hard wired connection to a data PBX. The user indicates the computer he or she wishes to be connected to, usually with a name or acronym, and the data PBX makes the connection. If all the connection points on the computer are busy, data PBX will hold the call in a queue and call the user back when the connection can be made. When the user no longer needs the connection, it is broken, and the hardware is available to another user.

Data PBXs are less expensive than PBXs. They can add an element of security to data connections by requiring a password before the connection to the computer is made.

Voice Mail

The public telephone system that handles voice messages has been around for over 100 years. Because this system is primarily a circuit switching system, it has one tremendous disadvantage. When the remote telephone is already in use or no one is present, the telephone call (the message) cannot be completed. Both voice mail and electronic mail overcome this disadvantage. During the next few years two of the major applications for data communications will be voice mail and electronic mail.

With regard to voice mail, great technical advances have occurred to make the telephone more accessible, easier to use, more attractive, and a true message switching system. Voice mail is a flexible means of sending a spoken message to someone even when the person is not at the remote terminal (the telephone). The sender speaks into the telephone, and the message is stored for later forwarding to its recipient. In effect, this turns the telephone system both into a message switching system (instead of circuit switching) and into a store and forward system.

Actually, voice mail is the transmission of a voice message to a recipient voice mailbox. Using a touchtone telephone with its standard 12-key dialing pad, the caller can record a message, listen to the message before transmitting it, and even change it if necessary. The message then can be sent to one or more recipients or even to a predefined group such as a department within a corporation or government agency. When it is convenient, the recipients check their voice mailboxes, scan to see who sent the incoming messages, and choose to listen to some now while saving others for later. Recipients can listen to the message, stop playing it if they are interrupted, skip ahead or back, or replay the message at will. After hearing the message, the recipient can generate a voice reply immediately and send it back to the person who sent the original message. Other options might be to forward the message to a third party and, of course, to discard the original message.

Voice mail has five major advantages over the traditional telephone. With voice mail it is no longer necessary to

— Place several calls to a person to find him or her near the telephone
— Move meeting schedules and match time zone differences around the world
— Place a number of calls to get a similar message to many different people
— Know where a person is located geographically to complete a call to the person (all you need to know is the voice mailbox number which he or she checks each day)
— Type your messages

With voice mail, the sender can place a call without interrupting the recipient, without having to know if the recipient is in the office or traveling around the world, and without regard to the time of day or night.

If a two-way information exchange is necessary because complex points must be discussed, then voice mail has a nice feature that can be used to set up a precise time, date, and telephone number to ensure that the connection can be made the first time. It is here that the newer telephones will have the most advantage because of their ability to transmit both voice and picture simultaneously. Video display telephones allow users to see the person with whom they are speaking (possibly for security reasons) and actually to show documents over the system.

Voice mail will be offered by the major telephone companies and special common carriers such as US Sprint and MCI.

Voice mail will be accepted more readily by general public telephone users than will electronic mail. This is because electronic mail requires, first, the ability to type and, second, access to a keyboard in order to type the text of a message. Professionally, teachers like to accept and transmit voice messages, whereas the ability to enter text messages must be learned as a special skill. More students can use their voice than can write a complete sentence correctly.

Incidentally, voice mail is achieved by digitizing a voice signal and breaking it into a stream of digital bits. Some systems are now capable of converting a voice signal into a digital bit stream of 4800 bits per second or even 2400 bits per second. This 2400 bits per second digital stream enables you to have four simultaneous voice conversations on a 9600 bits per second data communication circuit.

The number one advantage for voice mail is that everyone who currently has a touchtone telephone already has the terminal required to utilize this system and basically understands how this terminal (the telephone instrument) works.

Facsimile (FAX)

A facsimile (FAX) machine scans a sheet of paper electronically and converts the light and dark areas to electrical signals, which can then be transmitted over telephone lines. At the other end, a similar machine reverses the process and produces the original image on a sheet of paper. Individual characters are not sent as such; only as contrast between light and dark. As a result, the facsimile is ideal for sending preprinted documents or forms, as well as letters, contracts, and even photographs. Each facsimile machine therefore has two parts: a reader-transmitter and a receiver-printer.

Since the machine deals with light and dark areas (not letters, words, or numbers) any image, photograph, drawing, or graph can be transmitted. The facsimile machine scans back and forth across the original document in a series of scan lines. The most sophisticated facsimile machines can detect several shades of light or dark. The more shades detected, the more faithful the reproduction is at the receiving end. The speed to transmit and print an 8 1/2 x 11 document varies from 6 minutes to approximately 30 seconds, depending on the techniques used for transmitting.

Facsimile was invented in 1843, six decades before invention of the teletypewriter. Despite this early start, facsimile found little application for several decades. It first came into general use in the 1920s for transmitting wirephotos and weather maps and has been used extensively by law enforcement agencies for sending mug shots and fingerprints, but it has only recently gained acceptance as a communication machine.

Facsimile transmission has several advantages over other data communication methods in certain applications:

— If a document is already printed, it does not need to be rekeyed in order to be transmitted.
— Facsimile transmission conveys graphic as well as textual information.
— Facsimile transmission is less affected by transmission errors than data communications.
— Operation of facsimile machines is very simple and requires little training.
— Since the recipient receives an exact duplicate of the original image, graphs, charts, and handwritten notes can be sent as easily as typed documents. Generally, facsimile is used to transmit any document that must arrive quickly.

The Japanese have been leaders in the development of sophisticated facsimile machines. A large portion of the world's facsimile transmissions occur in Japan.

Videotex

Videotex is a relatively new application in which the computer is able to store text and images in digital form and transmit them to remote terminals for display or interaction.

Videotex pictures are scanned, interpreted, and stored on the computer in numerical format. Obtaining good quality pictures requires a large amount of disk space for the data representing the picture. Furthermore, the large amount of data may require several minutes to be transmitted to a terminal. Many users don't want to wait several minutes to see a simple picture. Scanning through a catalog would be virtually impossible. Fortunately, techniques are available to reduce the amount of data that must be stored and transmitted so that high-resolution pictures can be received in a reasonable amount of time. However, compared to data and text transmission, image transmission is still voluminous.

References

Amoto, Sam. (1991). T1 for Voice and Data Via Satellite. *Telecommunications*, April, 36-39.

Blyth, John and Blyth, Mary. (1985). *Telecommunications: Concepts, Development, and Management*. Mission Hills, CA: Glencoe Publishing Company.

Boker, Gabe. (1990). Teletranslating—Electronic File Transfer Via Domestic and International Data Communication. *Technical Communication*, August, 292-295.

Brodsky, Ira. (1991). *Wireless MANs/WANs Offer Data to Go*. Business Communication Review, February, 45-51.

DeNoia, Linda. (1987). *Data Communication: Fundamentals and Applications*. Columbus, OH: Merrill Publishing Company:

Green, James Harry. (1986). *The Dow Jones-Irwin Handbook of Telecommunications*. Homewood, IL: Dow Jones-Irwin.

Henderson, Warren. (1991). Testing High-Speed Modems—The Right Way. *Data Communication*, January, 82-86+.

Hindin, Eric. (1990). Satellite Network Does Data Transmission Right. Data Communication, October, 70+.

Mc Namara, John. (1982). *Technical Aspects of Data Communication*. 2nd ed. Bedford, MA: Digital Equipment Corp.

Mao, Leei. (1990). Computer Integrated Technology and Its Influence on Engineering Technology Programs. (ERIC Document Reproduction Service No. ED326716).

Mulqueen, John. (1990). Data Communications 1991 Market Forecast. *Data Communication.*, December, 95-98.

Owens, Ray. (1990). Computer-Based Technical Communication. *Technical Communication*, August, 297-298.

Chapter Five

Networking

Introduction

Educational applications are increasingly based on computers and communications. However, problems are raised by
distributed real-time computing. A network is a well-defined
collection of communications services. It is a controllable structure that ties together systems and components. Increasingly,
communications networks are used to draw together educational
information services. Whether in instruction or managing the
instruction, educational information is a vital resource.

The terms networking and network appear in the education
vocabulary with greater and greater frequency each year. The
information explosion in society, and particularly in education,
has both been fueled by and caused the technology explosion in
the field of telecommunications. Networking can be defined as
the ability to exchange information between users and share the
resources involved in this process.

There are many compelling reasons to consider the use of
educational networks. The mission of educational institutions is the
creation, storage, and dissemination of information. Communication
networks are tools to be used in accomplishing these tasks more
effectively, as they facilitate fast, reliable information exchange
and resource sharing.

101

Distributed Data Processing (DDP)

For the past forty years, new applications for computers have been presented and utilized by users. Educators have witnessed the advent and passing of several data processing organizations. The beginning of the computer revolution brought about a phase of data compilation and processing known as Electronic Data Processing (EDP), simple record-keeping systems. All clerical automation can be classified within this group. The characteristic of this application is its programmability. When operations are automated, there is no need for human intervention. Payroll is a good example of this process. Many schools have been utilizing this application for record keeping, reporting grades, inventory control, etc.

The unique feature of this system is *centralized data processing*. In this system all processing is done at a single computer center which provides all information services through a large computer system and supporting staff. This design may include input from remote locations but all processing and data storage are done at a single location. This data processing method was accepted because of the high cost of hardware and software, the shortage of data processing personnel, etc. Centralized processing, however, lacks flexibility and is less responsive to user needs. Also any disturbances at the central location create problems for the entire system. Centralized data processing organization does exercise centralized control, one advantage of this type of processing.

Problems associated with centralized data processing created another type of processing organization called *decentralized data processing*. As the name implies, data are processed in different locations. Naturally, this type possesses a high degree of responsiveness, however, lack of control and, in some cases, duplication of errors are probably the most serious shortcomings associated with decentralized processing.

Improvements in data communications and networking in the early 1970s made the third type of data processing organization a viable option. This type is usually called *distributed data processing (DDP)*. The processing power is simply distributed throughout the organization and communication links between the different locations are accomplished through the cooperative use of application software. Experts in the field believe a sound DDP system possesses the advantages of both centralized and decentralized systems by having decentralized processing with centralized control.

Another type of networking data processing system that has become very popular in recent years is called *Local Area Network (LAN)*. As it has been discussed earlier, LAN operates within a limited geographical distribution, such as a school or an organization. There is some overlap between DDP and LAN.

The type of data processing organization chosen depends on many factors. While centralized processing may work for one organization or school, it may not work for another. A careful and detailed analysis is needed in order to choose the right type of DDP organization.

One of the characteristics of network systems is resource sharing. By this we mean a computer can be shared by a group of users. In many organizations and schools LAN systems have been utilized to share components of a system, such as hard disk or a common database. Networking shows a lot of promise in educational computing. Through these systems students can access public databases for CAI purposes. Tutorial lessons and homework exercises can be installed for common access.

Networking can be very beneficial to the administrative side of educational computing as well. Office automation, electronic mail, and message distribution, examples of DDP systems, enhance productivity and effectiveness of administrators in public and private schools.

Though there are advantages in networking, we should be aware of some of the problems associated with distributed systems. Security is probably the biggest issue confronting users. When a system becomes a part of a DDP system, it is a target for computer hackers. Careful planning can aid in computer security. Computer security will be discussed in detail. Also, there are several technical problems associated with DDP systems. The compatibility issues between computer hardware and software is one of the common problems in DDP. The complexity associated with connecting these systems is another problem.

Considering the advantages and disadvantages of DDP, there is a clear indication of the real potential of these systems. With improvement of transmission speed, upgraded security measures, and enhancements in networking systems, DDP systems will be the trend of the future.

Network Topology

Network topology refers to the way computers in the network connect to one another. Several different network topologies exist, each with its own advantages and limitations. Among those topologies the most common types are *Star, Hierarchical, Ring,* and *Bus* networks.

Star Network

In star networks, a computer serves as a *central controller* and radiates communications outward to each connected computer or node. Figure 5.1 shows a star network. For two computers to send or receive data from one another, the data must be routed through the central controller. If the central controller becomes inoperable, all terminals or computers in the network cease to function. Only functions that can be handled independently by individual computers can continue. Another disadvantage of the star is that the central location may be bottlenecked under high traffic conditions. Star network is typically found in cases where a large-scale central computer is connected to many terminals in a time-sharing system. For example, many school systems have a large or medium-scale computer that handles administrative tasks, class scheduling, registration, and grading, as well as several terminals connected for instructional use.

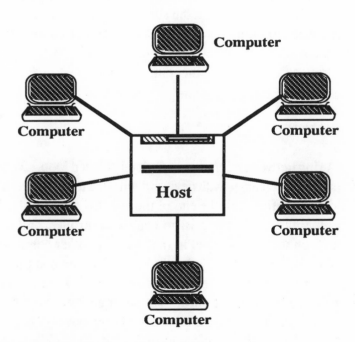

Figure 5.1. *Star Network*

Hierarchical Network

The hierarchical network, also known as *tree network* consists of a central computer to which several other computers are connected. Figure 5.2 illustrates a hierarchical network. The hierarchical network mirrors a typical organizational chart, and it is in this setting where a hierarchical configuration is most likely to be found. One can envision a school district office computer being connected to the local school computer and collecting data from it. The school district data can be consolidated with similar data from other school districts at the county level. Finally, all of the county data would be consolidated at the state level.

In this topology there is not a single point of failure in the network. Even if the node at the state level fails, the county and district can go on doing their daily processing and data transmission. Another advantage is of hierarchical topology in duty control and monitoring as well as implementing standards.

Ring Network

A ring network refers to a completely closed loop. A single communication channel, with devices connected to it, runs through a building or office until the end of the channel connects back to the beginning. Also, there is no central controller, and every computer on the ring is equal in rank to every other computer.

The data must travel around the ring to each computer in turn until they arrive at the desired computer. A ring may be unidirectioned or bidirectioned. An unidirectioned ring moves data in one direction only, a bidirectioned ring moves data in both directions, but in only one direction at a time. In a unidirectioned ring if one computer should break down, special software is

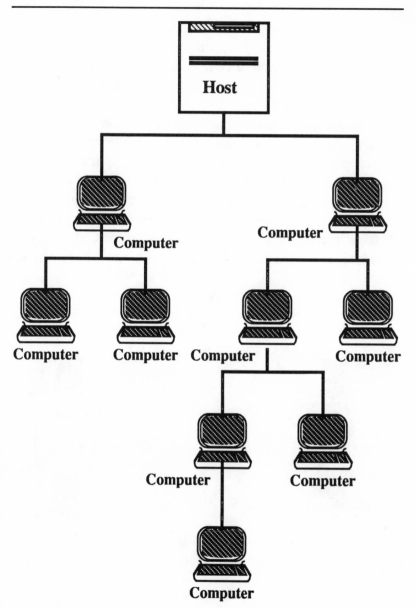

Figure 5.2. *Hierarchical Network*

required to keep the network functional. When one computer malfunctions in a bidirectional ring, a message can usually be sent in the opposite direction still allowing the computer to communicate with all the other active computers in the network. Figure 5.3 depicts a ring network.

This type of network could be used, for example, in a school setting where computers are located in different grade level classrooms. Each computer would handle the applications unique to its grade level. When sharing of data is required, the computers could pass data to one another over the ring network. For example, daily attendance information should be passed to the principal's office for inclusion in the daily statistics, or scheduling information could be passed on to the classroom by the principal's office.

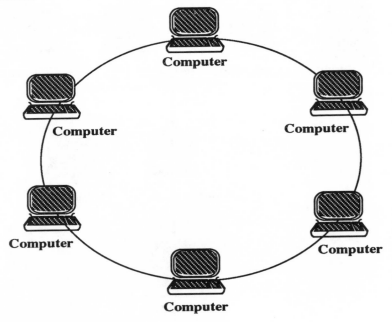

Figure 5.3. *Ring Network*

Bus Network

In the bus network, each computer is connected to a single communication cable via an interface; every computer can communicate directly with every other computer or device in the network. The beginning and end of the network do not connect, so a terminator must be placed at each end of the bus. Each connected device is given an address. To access a particular data a user just needs to know its address. In bus network, no central controller is necessary. All devices on the bus have equal rank. Figure 5.4 exhibits bus network.

A bus network is particularly popular as an internal connection technique for the various components of computers. It is convenient where computers and devices are spread throughout a school. A single communication channel can be run through classrooms and offices of a school. The bus network functions like a ring network in that each computer can handle independent processing tables and also communicate information to other computers.

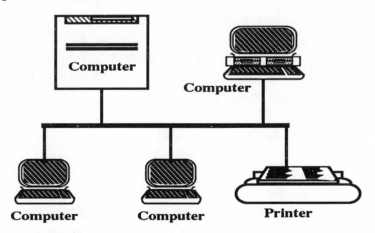

Figure 5.4. *Bus Network*

Hybrid Network

A hybrid network is a flexible or open-ended network concept that takes advantage of a mixture of different technologies or media to achieve a network. You can consider a hybrid network as any mixture of two or more network configurations combined. Hybrid networks may use a mixture of different types of transmission media (satellite, microwave, and so forth). Hybrid networks combine a variety of network environments and protocols into a single network, utilizing each network type's strong points to the fullest advantage. Figure 5.5 shows a hybrid network.

Bridge and Gateway

Connecting two networks together that operate according to the same ruler or *protocol* requires a device called a *bridge*. The bridge allows data to be sent off on one network and onto the other so that terminals on both networks can communicate as though a single network existed. If two networks operate according to different protocols, a device called a *gateway* is used to connect them. The gateway translates the protocols in order to allow computers on the two networks to communicate. Gateways may also provide the translation between the media and electrical specifications of two-device network.

Wide Area Network (WAN)

The wide area network (WAN) systems are too separated, either physically or geographically, to be included in a small in-house network. In other words WANs corner a much larger geographical area throughout than a LAN. They usually require the crossing of public rights of way, and use a common carrier

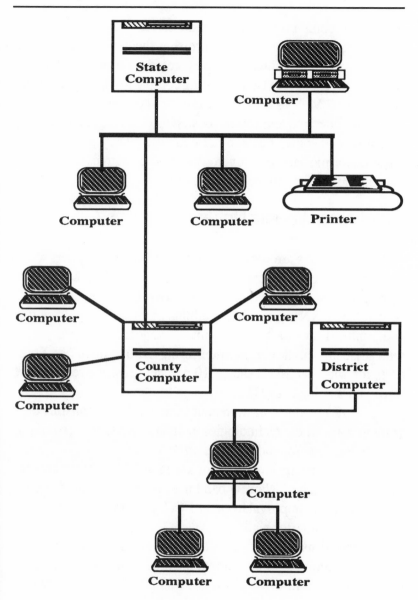

Figure 5.5. *Hybrid Network*

(telephone company). A common carrier is a government-regulated private company that furnishes the general public with communication facilities. The most noted examples of common carriers are AT&T, the Bell operating companies, US Sprint, MCI and so forth. WAN's use a broad range of communication media for interconnection and can be located as close together as a few blocks or as far away as another country. They generally use transmission media, such as microwave or satellite transmission, but they are not limited to these two forms.

Local Area Wireless Network

Most LANs are formed with a blend of twisted part wires (telephone wire), fiber optic cable, and coaxial cable. Local Area Wireless Network is another form of network topology. The idea of wireless LAN comes from cellular mobile phones in which geographical areas are divided into hexagonal shaped cells, with adjacent cells having noninterfering radio frequencies. Forecasts for wireless LANs show 210 percent growth over the next three years (Clegg, 1991).

There are three basic technologies used to transmit data without wire. These technologies include *spread spectrum radio, narrow band radio*, and *infrared light.*

Spread spectrum uses common radio frequencies and requires no licensing. Narrow band uses restricted radio frequencies and requires approval from the FCC. Both radio technologies can penetrate interior walls.

Infrared uses light waves as a transmission medium. No licensing is required to implement infrared technology, but there must be an open line of sight to accommodate the light signal.

The latest wireless LAN uses high-frequency radio transmissions. This unit is called Local Area Wireless Network (LAWN).

The hardware unit, about the size of a modem, attaches to an RS-232 port. This system is capable of handling two to twenty users. LAWN units can be placed up to 100 feet apart within a building and up to 500 feet apart between buildings. Each unit can act as a repeater, extending the total network length up to 300 feet indoors, through a maximum of two repeaters. The advantage of the wireless LAN might be that it runs on radio frequencies, thus eliminating the need for wire, cables, or optical fibers. Also, in the latest systems, there is no need for a file server and everyone communicates with everyone else.

Obviously, a disadvantage is the lack of security. To protect the privacy of messages, wires have to encrypt them before transmission.

Microcomputer Workstations

Microcomputer workstations are either general purpose microcomputers or specially designed input/output workstations that have custom-designed microprocessor chips. Many vendors have developed customized microcomputer workstations for use in office automation, data entry, the automated factory, banking, education, and a whole host of other special situations. The basic input/output device is a microcomputer. Its functions include editing data, possibly storing data, protocol conversion if required, mathematical calculations, and prompting for information or forms design (handled on the video screen); all can be handled locally without assistance from the host mainframe computer.

Technically, there is a difference between a workstation and a microcomputer. A workstation usually provides all of the tools that professionals need in their daily work. Among these tools are specialized applications like mathematical modeling, computer-assisted design (CAD), computer-assisted instruction, intensive programming, and networking. Today's workstation usually has more computing power than the average microcomputer. Workstations must offer true multitasking capability so that the user does not spend a large amount of time waiting for the computer to finish one job before starting the next one. On the other hand, a microcomputer may not have the ability to handle all of the specialized applications, and its multitasking ability may be significantly less. Most microcomputer users may be satisfied with printer spooling and telecommunications as a replacement for true multitasking capability. The primary use of a microcomputer is for a few functions such as word processing, drill and practice, tutoring, and spreadsheet modeling. As microcomputers get more powerful microprocessor chips, they will be as powerful as contemporary workstations. Therefore, today you may be able to see the difference between a workstation and a microcomputer, but tomorrow they may be the same thing.

Video Terminals

These terminals have a television screen and a typical typewriter keyboard. Sometimes they are called cathode ray tubes (CRT), video display units (VDU), or video display terminals (VDT). Alphanumeric video terminals are used in offices, whereas graphic video terminals are used by graphic designers. The intelligent version of a video terminal might be used for computer-assisted design.

In addition to a standard keyboard, the video terminal has a marker on the screen called a *cursor*. It moves about the screen to show students the next position in which a character will be printed.

When selecting a video terminal, you should consider what the transmitting line speed is, if users can rotate or tilt the screen for easy viewing, if split-screen mode is available so two or more screens can display simultaneously, whether the character matrix size is large enough for easy viewing, if a detachable keyboard would be advantageous, if a self-test mode is available, how many characters can be displayed horizontally and how many lines vertically, whether it can accommodate a separate printer that can be turned on and off as needed, and which editing functions are available such as character insertion/deletion, line insertion/deletion, erasing, and paging.

With regard to the individual student terminal, some specific items must be taken into account when you are ordering a video terminal. Because eyestrain and fatigue are the most common complaints of video terminal users, the following arrangements will increase productivity.

- A video tube screen filter should be obtained to protect the user from electromagnetic radiation, which can emanate as microwaves, infrared waves, and ultraviolet waves.
- An antiglare screen should be used to eliminate glare from the front face of the video tube. Glare is the number one complaint of people who use video terminals or micro-computers.
- Cursors should be visible from 8 feet away, and they should be seen easily at 3 feet. Sometimes it is advantageous to have the option of either a blinking cursor or a cursor that is on as a steady light.
- Detachable keyboards or a sloped keyboard may be desirable.
- Reverse video may ease eyestrain. With this feature, the student can change from a dark background with light characters to a light background with dark characters.
- Multiple colors also may reduce eyestrain.

- Adjustments for tube brightness, focus, and contrast are desirable to accommodate the variety of students who might use a video terminal.
- Glare and eyestrain can be reduced with the use of window shades, proper lighting, and movable screens that cut reflective glare.
- To prevent muscular aches and fatigue, VDTs should have movable keyboards, document holders, and screens that tilt to a comfortable viewing angle for the user. The height of the video screen and its ability to tilt might be critical to the student who wears bifocal lenses. Today's computer furniture often requires that video screens be placed above eye level. This consideration should be borne in mind when purchasing such furniture because students should be able to look down onto the screen.
- The characters on the video monitor tube should not jitter or flicker because this movement causes eyestrain. By using a magnifying glass to look at the characters, you should be able to determine whether they jitter or shake. Jitter is caused by an insufficient video reflection voltage which makes the electron beam inaccurate when refreshing the character. Flicker is caused by a fast decay of the phosphor and a slow refresh rate. Technically, you should accept nothing below 65 hertz (frequency). Many video data terminals are 45, 50, or 55 hertz, which does not provide a fast enough refresh rate to avoid noticeable or even subliminal flicker.
- Many users, however, feel that yellow/green tube color is the easiest to see and tends to reduce eyestrain. You should seriously consider purchasing video monitors that have multicolor capabilities because color tends to reduce eyestrain and enhances productivity. Color also is used to make it easier to understand an application.

- Students should always obtain the highest possible video monitor tube resolution. For example, some video monitors have resolution up to 800 (horizontal) by 560 (vertical) pixels. The higher the resolution (the greater number of pixels), the clearer the picture and the less eyestrain. (Pixels are "picture elements." Each one is a small dot on a video tube.)

Dumb and Intelligent Terminals

A dumb terminal does not participate in data control or data processing tasks. It usually does not have any internal storage for memory, nor does it have microprocessor chips; it has the bare minimum required to operate. The older, really dumb terminals transmitted asynchronously, and when a character was typed, the terminal transmitted the character immediately. Thus, central computer systems had to have receiving buffers for each of these terminals so that they could assemble the entire message before acting on it.

Integrated Services
Digital Networks (ISDN)

The Integrated Services Digital Network (ISDN) may supplant most of the communications networks we've come to know and hate. Traditional telephone systems and perhaps even cable-TV networks will wither away, to be replaced in our homes and offices by a super-sophisticated, all-purpose, multiplexed, high-speed digital "pipeline." An ISDN provides end-to-end digital connectivity to support a wide range of services, including voice and non-voice services, to which users have access by a limited set of standard multi-purpose user-network interfaces.

With the advent of ISDNs, all telecommunications will be affected digitally: telephones will conform to the new standard by digitizing voices and modems will become white elephants (or doorstops). For a start, ISDNs can be expected to carry voice, facsimile, computer data, and telex traffic, as well as support remote meter reading and the monitoring of fire and burglar alarms. Eventually, these networks may also carry TV broadcasts (displacing cable TV), video conferencing, security information, and probably other things nobody's even thought of yet. Widespread implementation of this exciting and terrifying technology is still a decade or two away, but preliminary steps are already being taken.

The idea of ISDN was brought into the world in the early 1970s by the CCITT, which has slowly been developing a set of standards for such networks. The CCITT was motivated by the realization that data transmission requirements would continue to grow rapidly and, in the absence of a standard, would be met in many divergent and incompatible ways. The ISDN concept is to create a uniform worldwide network of digital pathways and digital switches capable of transporting any form of data that can be reduced to bits, essentially any kind of communication. ISDN potentially integrates any and all communications services on a single standardized digital network. ISDNs promise:

— Pure end-to-end digital communications from anywhere to anywhere.
— An interface with worldwide standards for connectors, electrical signaling, and protocols.
— Compatibility with any and all types of communication, subject only to bandwidth limitations.
— Both circuit-switched connections (like dial-up telephone calls) and packet-switched connections.

— Seamless integration among all networks whose suppliers follow the ISDN standards.
— The flexibility to allow devices to interface with the network in intelligent ways, accommodating computers, for example, as something more than expensive telephone dialers.

Although it's too early for any guarantees to be made, ISDNs will probably open the door to very fast call setups, a universal physical connector, and universal methods of addressing subscribers and accounting for network usage, perhaps with a debit card accepted by every public phone on Earth. We can expect a feast of value-added features, starting with those described for PBXs in the previous chapter.

As a practical matter, it is likely that existing networks, primarily the international telephone network, will slowly evolve into ISDNs. Private ISDNs will also appear; indeed, several multinational corporations are already building them. Presumably, even these private networks will have some point of contact with the public ISDN.

ISDN Services

ISDNs provide two basic classes of service: *bearer services* and *teleservices*. In the case of bearer services, the network simply transports bits among users without concern for meaning. Two computers could use this low-level service for any data communication function. Teleservices are user-level services provided by a network itself. Familiar examples are voice telephony, Teletex (a modern version of telex), and facsimile transmission.

With ISDNs gradually taking over from the traditional phone system, the question of how customers on the old-style system will communicate with those on the new becomes very important. For voice, there is no problem. A typical voice call is frequently digitized today for at least some portion of its passage through the phone system. The codecs discussed earlier make voice ISDN compatibility a trivial concern. But what about data? How does a school computer with a 2,400-bps modem on an analog line communicate with the mainframe computer attached to an ISDN-style system? The general answer lies in the communication resource, a conversion component built into a PBX or central office switch.

ISDNs may be just around the corner, but their imminence has not depressed the market for devices, such as modems, that exploit traditional networks. Still, some modem manufacturers, notably Hayes Microcomputer Products, are busily engaged in the development of ISDN-related items.

Will ISDNs make communication less expensive? They might, because, among other things, service providers can get more utility out of existing plants by following ISDN practices. On the other hand, since communication services, especially for data, change so much with the coming of ISDNs, it's hard to compare what's available today with what one might expect tomorrow. In any event, ISDN, like most technical breakthroughs of the past 50 years, will undoubtedly become less expensive as the technology matures.

ISDNs hold the promise of speed and services that may seem luxurious compared to what we are accustomed to. But, all too quickly, we'll get used to them, and cry out for evermore bandwidth. In the mid to late 1990s, we may see the introduction of wideband ISDNs operating at hundreds of megabits per second. This second-tier service will depend on replacing copper wire with optical fibers in local loops. The hard part, however, is switching lots of connections at such lightning speeds.

References

Angier, Jennifer and Hoehl, Susan. (1986). Local Area Networks (LAN) in the Special Library. *Online*, November, 19-36.

Azarmsa, Reza and Byrd, Gary. (1988). Microcomputer Networking in an Inexpensive Way. *TechTrends*, September, 28-29.

Barden, Robert and Golden, Richard. (1986). Networking and Telecommunications on Campus: A Tutorial. *EDUCOM Bulletin*, Summer, 18-25.

Bishop, Ann. (1990). The National Research and Education Network (NREN): Promise of New Information Environment. (ERIC Document Reproduction Service No. ED327219).

Brienne, Deborah and Goldman, Shelley. (1989). Networking: How It Has Enhanced Science Classes in New York Schools . . . And How It Can Enhance Classes in Your School, Too. *Classroom Computer Learning*, April, 44-53.

Clegg, Peter. (1991). LAN Times Lab Tests Wireless LANs. *LAN Times*. July 8, 79.

Crume, Charles, and Maddux, Cleborne. (1990). Educational Computer Networks: An Overview. *Educational Technology*, July, 26-30.

Davis, Linda. (1989). Networking on Campus. *Video Systems*, October, 88-92.

Julyan, Candace. (1989). National Geographic Kids Network: Real Science in the Elementary Classroom. *Classroom Computing Learning*, October, 30-39.

Kenderdine, John and Hull, Ann. (1988). Your Computer, My Computer, Let's Network. *The Science Teacher*, March, 40-41.

Lavin, Richard and Phillipo, John. (1990). Improve School-based Management Through Intelligent Networking. *T.H.E. Journal*, November, 69-71.

Lefkon, Dick. (1987). A LAN Primer. *Byte*, July, 147-165.

Lehrer, Ariella. (1988). A Network Primer: When Is a Network Not a Network? *Classroom Computer Learning*, February, 39-46.

Lehrer, Ariella. (1988). A Network Primer: How They're Used . . . And How They Could Be Used. *Classroom Computer Learning*, April, 41-47.

McCarthy, Robert. (1989). The Advantages of Using a Network. *Electronic Learning*, September, 32-38.

Mason, Robin. (1989). The Use of Computer Network for Education and Training. Report to the Training Agency. (ERIC Document Reproduction Service No. ED327163).

Chapter Six

Computer-Mediated Communications

Introduction

Data communication can bring the world into the classroom. Properly structured and facilitated within the existing curriculum, instructional telecommunications can be a powerful tool in the instructional arsenal. It can improve critical thinking skills and help us reevaluate concepts that may ultimately lead to true global education.

Engaging students in a computer-mediated dialogue as the medium of exchange can be a motivating and enriching experience. Data communication allows an individual student, or class of students, to discuss and share experiences with unlimited others. The physical distance between students becomes unimportant, because telephone lines stretch across the country and around the world. Telecommunications have some significant advantages over the more conventional models of exchanging information. With telecommunications, an open letter to a very large audience is possible, inviting any number of responses.

There are several kinds of computer-mediated communications, among those are electronic mail (E-mail), bulletin board systems, computer conferencing, and online database.

Electronic Mail

Electronic mail, E-mail for short, is a service that allows users to leave text-form messages and send letters or documents from terminals to a central data file for later retrieval by the recipient, entering access and identification codes. In a typical application, a user with a microcomputer and modem types a message and then identifies the recipient(s) with identification numbers or names. There are two general types of electronic mail: an in-house network, which connects all or some of the teachers or students within a school or district, and an external network connecting people at different locations around the world.

In some local area networks, the message is sent directly to a microcomputer with an automatic answering capability and stored in a file to await disposition. In other networks, the message can be stored in the system's centralized electronic mailboxes to await attention or is posted to an electronic bulletin board for any user to access.

Characteristics of E-mail

— E-mail does not create written documents although users can have messages printed if they wish.
— E-mail enables users to avoid at least some telephoning. This eliminates busy signals, dealing with intermediate secretaries, leaving messages, or playing telephone tag.
— E-mail is usually much faster than any postal delivery since messages are sent electronically and therefore received almost instantaneously. This advantage is important for long distance communications that involve up-to-the-minute information.

— It is less expensive and faster to prepare and send a single message sent simultaneously to multiple addresses.
— In many circumstances, E-mail is cheaper than phoning, as well as more convenient.
— E-mail enables users to time-shift messages, that is, to send messages quickly to distant time zones without both parties being awake.
— E-mail can be used for mass distribution. This is accomplished by using computerized lists of recipients, for example, all of the elementary teachers in a district, state, or nation.

E-mail can be used in many classrooms and even between classrooms. Teachers can generate ideas for electronic mail in class discussions. To get students interested, teachers can start with the following topics:

— **Reviews.** Critical discussions of movies, books, records, software, or television shows.
— **Whimsy.** Collection of jokes, anecdotes or riddles.
— **Recipes.** Favorite recipes and comments about recipes shared.
— **News.** Discussion of current events.
— **Trivia.** Trivia questions asked and answered.
— **Writing.** Poems, essays and short stories by students.
— **Improve it.** A sentence or paragraph with errors in it; students reply with a list of the errors found.
— **Story.** Additions to a continually growing story.
— **Field trips.** Writing about field trips and interesting attractions.
— **Clubs.** Announcements of club meetings and activities.
— **Classes.** Recommendations on classes to take; discussions of class projects.

— **Sales**. Information about local store sales.
— **Want ads**. Things to sell or things wanted.
— **Special events**. Sporting events; birthday greetings.

With a little time and effort, teachers can create an electronic mail system that provides students with an exciting environment in which to write and exchange ideas.

However, electronic mail does have some drawbacks:

— It is expensive to set up, and if used indiscriminately, it can be expensive to operate.
— There is no guarantee that electronic mail systems will be compatible.
— There is also the problem of privacy and security of electronic mail. It is difficult to ensure that only the recipient reads the mail.
— Electronic "junk mail" has emerged.

Bulletin Board Systems (BBS)

A BBS is essentially an electronic equivalent of a conventional bulletin board. Many BBS's are established as a way for users to exchange information about any topic. Although features vary among BBS's, most provide the user with the ability to post messages for other users, to read messages posted by other callers, and to communicate with the system operator (sysop).

The sysop is a person who operates the bulletin board, asks questions about the BBS's operation, reports problems, makes suggestions, posts notices of equipment or services for sale, and uploads and downloads programs. Most BBS's are operated by individuals who have an interest in computers and communication and who have a desire to share information with others. But hardware manufacturers, software publishers, other businesses, and schools have also started bulletin boards. For example, Parker Brothers, a game company, set up such a bulletin board for its customers to order replacement parts for games such as Monopoly.

The bulletin board requires its own telephone line; the computer is plugged into that line and left on 24 hours a day. The appropriate software allows the bulletin board computer to automatically answer telephone calls from other computers, accept and store messages from outside users, and allow access to the information stored in its files.

Most BBS's currently in operation are noncommercial and free of charge. The telephone company, however, charges for long distance phone time that may be used when communicating with a BBS.

There are two basic types of BBS's: message-only and file transfer. Message-only systems allow public or private messages to be sent and received and public bulletin boards to be viewed.

The file transfer systems allow files to be uploaded and downloaded. Public-domain software can be downloaded from BBS's. These files may include games, application software, and system utilities.

Schools may use a BBS for many reasons. This function operates during the day. During the night, however, the bulletin board dials other electronic bulletin boards to exchange electronic mail and other student writing.

Some Functions of BBS

A BBS provides easy and inexpensive ways to share information. Some of the examples are:

— Posting school announcements, class schedules, and student activity programs.

— On-line conferencing between teachers and students. This method allows students and teachers to communicate without meeting by appointment at a designated time and place.
— Exchanging of public domain software is possible.
— Posting general information and swap shop type bulletins.
— Parent-teacher conferencing can be established.
— Announcing employment opportunities for students.
— Posting fund-raising activities.

BBS's are vulnerable to abuse, such as problems with censorship, obscenity, loss or damage of materials, and copyright and privacy issues. Also, callers can tie up the bulletin board for long periods of time. The sysop (systems operator) should be aware of these forms of abuse in order to develop strategies to prevent misuse.

Computer Conferencing

Computer conferencing consists of communication terminals used by participants to access a central computer. The central computer stores text entered by the sender and forwards the information to the recipients when they call the computer. In one respect, computer conferencing is similar to electronic mail. The difference is that instead of thinking in terms of mail boxes, the user should think in terms of file folders. For each participant there would be a file folder. In addition, file folders can be assigned to topics.

Computer conferencing is a means of facilitating communication among people or organizations which are geographically remote from one another but which are linked by their research interests and activities.

Computer conferencing is a technological development that will enable educational researchers to work more efficiently and quickly. In education it can be a valuable tool in grant-proposal writing since several participants from different institutions could contribute.

Characteristics of Computer Conferencing

- Computer conferencing is interactive.
- It can be combined with other types of teleconferencing to enhance its effects.
- Sessions can be private and restrict participants.
- Computer conferences don't require that everyone participate at the same time.
- Computer conferences can provide a written record, or "hard copy," of all communications.
- There are no time restrictions; people can participate at any time of the day or night.
- Individuals may participate from home or office.
- Communications, messages, and information can be kept available online, providing a complete and accurate record of all activity.

Applications of Computer Conferencing

Seminars. Computer conferencing is used to provide courses, in-service education, and other seminars to individuals around the corner and around the globe. Such seminars are becoming common. The interaction opportunity between seminar participants and faculty leaders transcends the conventional classroom. The exchange of information, reaction, experiences and nuances of interpretation are possible.

These aspects of computer conferencing have led to the "electure," or electronic lecture. It is now common for experts in various fields to "go online" at a predetermined time to address some area of their expertise. Comments from the audience are responded to and issues debated. These electures can be one session or ongoing.

Regular seminars by university scientists and industry experts are held on CompuServe's Science Education Forum. These seminars allow students of all ages to interact with experts in a way not otherwise possible.

Workshops. Writing and programming workshops have been held online where members of the "conference" all contribute to a final product. When a very accurate record of all activities is required, computer conferencing provides it. Some conferencing systems provide automatically timed, dated, and identified-by-contributor transactions that are immediately retrievable.

Staff Meetings. When a project's staff is dispersed around the globe and discussions of highly technical material need to take place, computer conferencing is the communication vehicle of choice. It eliminates distance and time-zone barriers.

Conferencing. Computer conferences may have many concurrent sessions arranged by topic or purpose, just like a traditional face-to-face conference. Each group may establish a forum that in turn can create several subconferences. A computer forum might have subconferences for people with a special interest in a specific brand of computers (e.g., Apple, IBM, or Kaypro), or in a specific software package (e.g., WordStar, Lotus 1-2-3, or Symphony), or it might be divided by purpose (e.g., project management, organization planning, or problem solving).

Standard Classroom Activities. Students can collaborate on class themes or correct each other's math homework. The computer allows students, teachers, and other educators to unite over time and distance. For example, Modern American History is taught in a new way at the Rochester Institute of Technology. Off-campus students can participate in class discussions through computer conferencing. The professor used personal computers and modems to send and receive electronic mail on the mainframe. The students evaluated the course. The results showed the computer conferencing course graded above average (Coombs, 1988).

Information Exchanges. Technical information can be stored online and used by people with conflicting viewpoints to bring about solutions to ongoing problems. Continuing dialogue between experts, problem solvers, and field personnel can be maintained around the city or around the globe.

Evaluation/Research. The ability to conduct and analyze surveys online and to network independent research groups allows geographically dispersed groups to conduct and maintain otherwise impossible research activities. The Texas Association of School Boards (TASB) has been able to use the Electric Pages to survey its districts and provide information for reports to the legislature.

Public Service Meetings. Statewide mandates from legislatures may stimulate community efforts across the state, and the problems that arise in one locale are likely to arise in another. Computer conferencing can be used to solve problems involved in the implementation of educational policies. For example, the education reform bills force school districts to develop specific plans regarding discipline. Conferencing schools and districts, they can learn much from each other. Computer conferences are also used to rapidly survey the membership of geographically dispersed groups for lobbying purposes or to formulate other action.

Benefits of Computer Conferencing

There are many advantages to computer conferencing, and the potential future benefits are staggering. It could lead to global networks, the possibility of expanding our biological intelligence to form a hyperintelligence—an intelligence operating on a global scale and representing a major evolutionary step for our society and our education. Computer conferencing is here now and it has already brought with it some major advantages over other types of communication and conferencing. Some of the advantages are:

Allows students to catch up: Students can join a computer conference at any time and, in a very short time, immediately catch up on everything that's happened. Most importantly, this is accomplished without disruption.

Speeds communication: Computer conferencing is immediate. To start the conference, there is no need for a quorum.

Increases productivity: Individuals can instantly create hard copies of online activities. Computer conferences also usually have online databases of relevant materials. This provides a participant with instant access to potentially vast amounts of organized materials.

Eliminates travel: Worldwide educators and experts can come together online and provide information to students, all without involving a single mile of travel. Conferences also provide necessary training for urban teachers without a single teacher having to face traffic.

Saves money: It is axiomatic that if computer conferencing can provide all of the above benefits, it must also save money. Even though long-distance charges and system surcharges can be expensive, airfare, the cost of hotels, food, rental cars, conference rooms, and other related costs are much higher.

Eliminates scheduling and time zone problems: Since in most cases "real-time" conferencing is not necessary, participants can log on to the system whenever they like and catch up on everything that is going on. Real-time conferencing can take place from anywhere, so if participants have to meet with someone from another time zone at 3:00 a.m., at least they can do it from their own home.

Allows longer communications: Because participants participate when they want or need to and because the costs are considerably less than those of traditional conferences, it is possible to have a conference that lasts for the duration of the interest of its members. This may be especially useful for interorganizational arrangements during project collaborations. For example, colleges of education, state education agencies, and school districts could collaborate on preparing teachers to meet new state mandates and provide experts online from the various relevant agencies.

Provides hardcopy documentation: Messages, agendas, communications of all kinds, and even databases usually remain in a conference "area" until they are removed by the authorized coordinator. Material can be accessed by all authorized members and read, printed, or "downloaded" to disk for later use. Material is usually dated, timed, and identified by author as it is entered on the system. This feature is especially significant for decision-making activities.

Provides flexibility: Computer conferences combine the best features of a conference call with those of electronic mail and networks.

It is topic driven: Large conferences are often topic, not person, driven. This means that participants can use the telephone in conjunction with their computer to contact a conference full of people who are concerning themselves with a specific topic, instead of using the phone in the traditional manner to call individually on persons who may or may not be available or interested. Most large national and international computer information utilities have numerous ongoing conferences on everything from cooking to lasers. Now, instead of meeting with the local tropical fish society once a month, users may meet on-line with fish enthusiasts every night, if they so desire.

On-line Database

A well-designed on-line database system allows users to ask a computer to find only information that is relevant to their needs. A variety of databases exist, each specializing in a particular topic or type of information. There are three general types of databases: full text, bibliographic, and non-bibliographic.

The full text systems provide complete copies of documents such as news articles, research reports, and software evaluations. Typical of these is NEXIS, run by Central Data Services. The complete text of every *Washington Post, Newsweek, U.S. News and World Report* and several other periodicals resides in its computer. The newspaper articles date from 1977 and the magazines from 1975.

Bibliographic databases hold references to the original report or article rather than the full text. These banks are usually searched using key words, terms which are selected as appropriately describing the subject of the document when the reference is entered.

The most useful of the bibliographic databases to educators is probably the Educational Resources Information Center (ERIC), which is sponsored by the U.S. Department of Education. With ERIC, key words can be combined to target an exact topic. For example, you might combine the words "junior high," and "reading" to find articles on teaching reading to seventh graders. After receiving the references, it would be up to you to locate the original articles. Fortunately, users will be guided by relatively short descriptions of the references to help them decide if they even want to locate the journals or microfiche with the actual articles.

The greatest disadvantage of a bibliographic database is that the indexer must accurately determine the content of each article. An article on special education, for example, might contain a section on gifted education. Unless the indexer noticed that reference, the article would not be discovered in your search for information on the GATE (gifted and talented education) program.

Non-bibliographic databases are simply collections of data. The Bureau of Labor Statistics, for example, maintains the BLS Data bank in which you might find salaries for various occupations in various states.

Most of these databases allow you to customize the reports you receive to some extent. The BLS system uses the TPL (Table Producing Language) to simplify selecting and displaying of information from those files.

Searching a computer database involves at least three entities: the information owner who has gathered and entered the information into the computer; the database vendors, or organizations which contract with information owners and may charge a subscription fee and fee for search time; and the use of telephone lines to access the database system.

Computer-Mediated
Communication in Education

Over the last few years, there has been a rapid increase in the use of the computer in delivering instruction. Computer-mediated communication has opened a broad range of alternatives for learning.

Arias and Bellman (1990) state that there is strong evidence to suggest that the delivery of courses using computer mediated communication as an interactive technology is particularly relevant to resolving many of the problems for effectively reaching and educating culturally and linguistically diverse students and other nontraditional learners. In their article, they discuss an experimental project using computer communications in seven universities in the Southwest and six academic and research institutions in Mexico to present how this technology is viable for these purposes.

The project is known as BESTNET, which is an acronym for the Binational English and Spanish Telecommunications Network, and involves the use of computer conferencing. The technology allows faculty to interact with students at a number of dispersed sites located in high target population concentration areas as well as offer special seminars and courses involving collaborative teaching by faculty at different institutions.

The use of computer conferencing for online and distance education has become an accepted delivery system over the past five to seven years. There are now educational host conferencing systems at universities in the United States, Canada, Britain, Ireland, France, Sweden, Japan and, to a limited extent, the former Soviet Union. Students log on to a host computer either at their university or by accessing a data packet switching network. They then download all waiting items in one or more computer conferences for the class. (Arias and Bellman, 1990)

Computer-mediated communication increases the quality of papers written by students. Cohen and Riel (1989) state that computer networks make it possible to increase the range of goals and audiences for students' writing and in doing so may provide a first step in the reintegration of students into the larger society.

Carnegie-Mellon University announced its entry into electronic learning environments with the system called Andrew. Carnegie-Mellon University leaders expect Andrew to have a major positive impact on the institution by supporting computer-aided instruction, the method used in professional work, communication among students and faculty, and information access and delivery (Scigliano, 1988).

The computer-based programs at Nova University began in the Fall of 1983, and depend heavily on microcomputers, modems, and telecommunication networks in conjunction with a supermini computer host. Students from 26 different states, including Alaska, conduct their online classwork in coordination with lecturers that teach the seminars.

In all these computer-based programs, students work extensively at home preparing assignments and projects for transmission online. They also contact their professors online and participate in electronic conferences (Scigliano, 1988).

New Jersey Institute of Technology (NJIT) constructed a prototypical Virtual Classroom, offering many courses fully or partially on-line. Students and professors, using personal computers, communicate with each other through online computer communication. The conclusions reached from the Virtual Classroom project were that learning outcomes were at least as good as outcomes from traditional face-to-face courses. The average student who participated in the on-line experiment felt that both access to and quality of the educational experience were improved. (Kaye and Others, 1989).

The Center for Distance Learning of Empire State College (New York) offers a course in contemporary American diplomacy entirely through the use of computer conferencing and electronic mail. The computer is used to create a learning environment where course participants can interact with each other and with the instructor, thus overcoming the isolation of the independent learner. In the three months the pilot has been online, it has demonstrated that computer conferencing can extend many of the learning opportunities of the classroom to distance and independent study. In addition, the written work submitted by members of this course was found to be superior, both as to breadth of research and quality of analysis, to work submitted by a previous non-computer class.

It has been concluded that, rather than diminishing the intensity and flexibility of learning on one's own, computer conferencing enhances independent study by providing peer interaction. (Roberts, 1987).

Research has shown that the effects of computer-mediated communication systems have been both positive and negative. Positively, they have helped to augment oral communication. Negatively, they have a detrimental impact on organizational communication structures. For example, some studies have shown that these technologies have bureaucratized organizational structure and shifted power to those who control computer resources. The importance of computer-mediated communication is not so much its impact on information processing but its impact on the structure of organizations. Organizational researchers should examine how computer-mediated communication systems become paralleled, integrated, opposed, or useful to the larger organization culture. Also, they should analyze how individuals interact with computer-mediated communication machines and networks to define their role (Hacker, 1986).

References

Arias, Armando and Bellman, Beryl. (1990). Computer-Mediated Classrooms for Culturally and Linguistically Diverse Learners. In Faltis and DeVillar, Ed. *Language Minority Students and Computers.* New York: The Haworth Press.

Batt, Russell H. (1989). The Computer Bulletin Board. *Journal of Chemical Education,* August, A198-A201.

Brienne, Deborah and Goldman, Shelley. (1989). Networking: How It Has Enhanced Science Classes in New York Schools . . . and How It Can Enhance Classes in Your School, Too. *Classroom Computer Learning,* April, 45-53.

Cohen, M. and Riel, M. (1989). The Effect of Distant Audiences on Students' Writing. *American Educational Research Journal,* February, 143-159.

Coombs, Norman. (1990). Computing and Telecommunications in Higher Education: A Personal View. *Educational Technology,* February, 46-47.

Coombs, Norman. (1988). History by Teleconference. *History Microcomputer Review,* Spring, 37-39.

Gallagher, Brian. (1989). VideoTechnology: Its Effect on Teaching English and Film. *Education Digest,* March, 29-32.

Gersten, R., Carnine, D., and Woodard, J. (1987). Direct Instruction Research: The Third Decade. *Remedial and Special Education,* June, 48-56.

Hacker, Kenneth. (1986). *Organizational Culture and the Design of Computer-Mediated Communication Systems: Issues for Organizational Communication Research.* (ERIC Document Reproduction Service No. ED278082).

Hunter, Beverly. (1990). *Computer-Mediated Communications Support for Teacher Collaborations: Researching New Contexts for Both Learning and Teaching.* (ERIC Document Reproduction Service No. ED321733).

Kaye, Tony, et al. *Computer Conferencing in the Academic Environment*. (ERIC Document Reproduction Service No. ED320540).

Kelly, Luke and Zuckerman, Michael. (1990). Telecommunications-Electronic Mail. *Journal of Physical Education, Recreation and Dance*, Spring, 86-89.

Koorland, M. A. (1990). Telecommunications Skills Training for Students with Learning Disabilities: An Exploratory Study. *Educational Technology*, January, 34-36.

Roberts, Lowell. (1987). *The Electronic Seminar: Distance Education by Computer Conferencing*. (ERIC Document Reproduction Service No. ED291358).

Romiszowski, Alexander and de Haas, Johan. (1989). Computer Mediated Instruction: Using E-Mail as a Seminar. *Educational Technology*, October, 7-14.

Rye, Jell-Jon. (1988). Technology Learning Activities Motivate Students. *Education Digest*, October, 49-51.

Sayers, Dennis and Brown, Kristin. (1987). Bilingual Education and Telecommunications: A Perfect Fit. *The Computing Teacher*, April, 23-24.

Schug, Mark C. (1988). Computers in High School Social Studies. *Education Digest*, November, 23-26.

Sciglino, John, et al. (1988). *An On-Line Classroom for the Unix Environment*. (ERIC Document Reproduction Service No. ED320585).

Vlahakis, Robert. (1988). From TASS to Tallahassee: In Search of Today's News. *Classroom Computer Learning*, May/June, 82-87.

Wasson, Lynn E. (1990). Electronic Mail: Teaching It by Using It. *Business Education Forum*, January, 15-17.

Chapter Seven

Teleconferencing

Introduction

Electronic meetings, convened across a nation or around the world, can be beneficial as well as cost effective. Every day hundreds of teleconferences are held in different sites and thousands of interested groups share information, asking questions via telephone line, eliminating the need to travel a long distance or, in some instances, leave the office. Soon after the first communication satellite, Telstar 1, launched into a geosynchronous orbit on July 1962, a multi-billion-dollar industry started. The satellite communications income for 1989 exceeded $62.5 million and the returned revenue for 1989 was 15.2 percent (Standard & Poor's, 1991).

The teleconferencing industry expected total sales (worldwide) of more than $485 million in 1986 and was projected to total over $3.7 billion in 1990 (Teleconference Sep./Oct., 1986). Satellite communication services expected to rise from $800 million in 1990 to around $1 billion by 1992 (U.S. Department of Commerce, 1991).

Teleconferencing has been applied to business, education, medicine, news, military, NASA, agriculture, art, and state and federal government for some time. The business and marketing communities are using video conferencing to meet a broader range of needs than ever before. Today teleconferencing has even gone beyond international borders. In spring 1985, for example, Compaq Computer Corporation decided to hold its annual stockholders meeting and new product announcement simultaneously in Houston, Chicago, Dallas, Los Angeles, San Francisco, New York, and Washington D. C.. Beyond those, the conference also was to go to Toronto, London, Paris, and Munich. In all, approximately 3,000 people attended the 90-minute teleconference.

How It All Started

In 1945 Arthur C. Clarke, a science fiction writer, published an article in *Wireless World*, a British publication. Clarke suggested a global communications system using three satellites placed in geosynchronous orbit at equal distance from each other. Clarke assumed that these three satellites would appear motionless if they orbited the earth at the same speed as the earth's rotation. Because of Clarke's line of work, this idea was not well received in the scientific community. After all, even the transatlantic telephone was a decade in the future.

In the late 1950s, the notion of satellite communications systems motivated group of scientists at the Bell Laboratories to develop a non-geosynchronous satellite communications system called Telstar 1. This first American communication satellite weighed only a few dozen pounds, and was placed in low orbit on July 10, 1962, from Cape Canaveral by a modified Thor-Delta rocket. Because of the low orbit, a massive antenna was needed and continuous communications were impossible. Today satellites are placed in geosynchronous orbit 22,300 miles over the equator. The satellites are at least 180 miles, or 2 to 5 degrees, apart. Any closer would cause microwave beams from adjacent satellites to interfere with each other. Satellites orbit at the exact speed that the earth rotates, so the satellites can always be found at a specific location in the sky. This orbit is called the Clarke Belt in honor of Arthur Clarke.

Types of Teleconferencing

Teleconferencing can occur between two locations (point to point) or between several different locations (point to multipoint).

Teleconferencing can use any one of several formats: one-way video/two-way audio, two-way audio/two-way video, picturephone, two-way audio, and computer conferencing.

One-way video/two-way audio is the most common format. Video and audio signals originate from a TV station or a mobile unit, the signals are transmitted to a communications satellite in orbit and then down linked to an earth station (satellite dish), and the teleconference participants.

The participants are encouraged to interact through a direct phone line. The audience can be heard but not seen at the point of origin.

Two-way audio/two-way video is more expensive and mostly used by the television networks. In this format participants are in different locations and can both see and hear one another. The audio and video signals from both sites are transmitted via satellite and received by satellite dish.

Picturephone teleconferencing is slightly different from two-way audio-video. In this format, the phone line is used to send the video and audio signals. Because of band width limitations, the image is not in full motion. Still images are sent in every few seconds via satellites, microwaves, landlines or other means. The audio, however, is normal. Recent advancement in technology has improved picturephone teleconferencing quality.

Computer conferencing consists of communication terminals used by participants to access a central computer. The central computer stores text entered by the sender and forwards the information to the recipients when they call the computer. In one respect, computer conferencing is similar to electronic mail. The difference is that instead of thinking in terms of mail boxes, the user should think in terms of file folders. For each participant there would be a file folder. In addition, file folders can be assigned to topics. Computer conferencing in education could be a valuable tool in grant proposal writing since several participants from different institutions could contribute. For more information see chapter 6.

The most inexpensive teleconferencing format is *two-way audio* teleconferencing. It is estimated that about 90 percent of the teleconferences are audio conferences. Information is received via phone line and amplified through a speaker phone. The responses are sent from microphone via phone line. This format is effective when individuals know one another and the information to be discussed is not visual.

Video signals are transmitted on broadband since they require a wider band because of the nature of the signal and the amount of the information in a television picture.

A transmission line called *T1* is used to transmit at a rate of 1.544 million bits of information per second. The T1 line can carry videoconferences, phone calls, and data, concurrently. Video transmission is very expensive, however, by compressing the signals video conferencing is becoming more affordable.

A codec (coder-decoder) device takes the standard, analog T.V. signal, converts it to a digital data stream, and compresses it by up to 99%. The signals are then decoded at the receiving end. This compression enables cost effective transmission of two-way videoconferencing (Compression Labs, Inc.).

Uplink and Downlink

Videoconference signals usually consist of an uplink from a TV station or mobile transmitter and a downlink to a receiving satellite dish. In an uplink, the signals changes to 6 giga hertz(GHz) through an up convertor. A power amplifier amplifies the wattage of signals and leads to the antenna, where the signals are converted to narrow beam for better penetration. Finally, the satellite receiver 22,300 miles away receives the signals.

In a downlink, the satellite converts the incoming signals to 4 giga hertz (GHz) and sends the signal to the transmitting antenna. The signals are received by the earth stations (TVRO, CATV, homeowner dish). The signals are picked up by the dish and reflected to the feedhorn in the middle of the dish. The feedhorn is in the focal point of the dish. Low-noise amplifiers (LNA) boost weak signals and the downconverter converts signals to TV signals (70 MHz). The converted signals pass through a coaxial cable to a satellite receiver. The video signals are processed in the satellite receiver and sent to a TV set for display. Figure 7.1 illustrates the uplink and downlink process.

Video signals received by satellite are bipolar, horizontal and vertical polarity. Polarization refers to the technique used that allows two different signals to be sent from a single transponder (receiver and transmitter) on each satellite. Overlapping frequencies will not interfere with one another if one signal is broadcast on a vertical plane and the other on a horizontal plane. Each communication satellite is capable of handling 24 channels, 12 horizontal and 12 vertical. Each satellite transponder may be used to carry any of the following:

— one color television channel with program sound
— 1200 voice channel

22,300 Miles

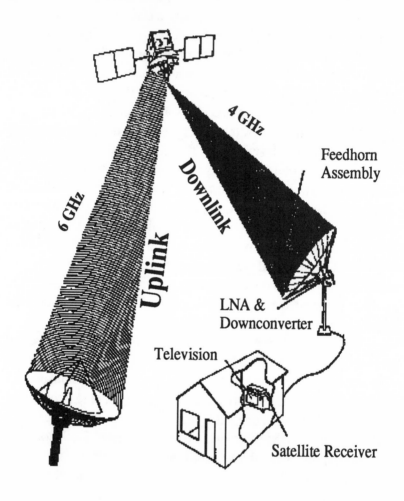

Figure 7.1. *Satellite Uplink and Downlink*

— a data rate of 50 megabytes per second (Mbps)
— the center 24 Mhz of each band may relay either:
    16 channels of 1.544 Mbps, or
    400 channels of 64,000 bps, or
    600 channels of 40,000 bps

A major advantage of satellite transmission is its declining cost. In 1965 the investment cost was $23,000 per voice channel per year. Today it is in the region of $60 per voice channel per year. Likewise, the cost of earth stations are declining. The first earth station constructed for Telstar cost in excess of $10 million. Now, a powerful earth station receiver only costs between $1,000 to $4,000, depending on the size of the receiving dish.

C-Band and KU-Band

Microwave frequencies begin at about 1,000 Mhz (1 giga-hertz) and rise in frequency. Communication satellites operate at microwave frequencies. C-band communication satellites, used by most satellite programmers, operate within the 3.7 to 6 GHz frequency band. Figure 7.2 shows C-band communication satellites. KU-band operates within the range of 11 to 14 GHz. The Federal Communications Commission (FCC) designated the lower portion of the KU-band (11.7 to 12.2 GHz) as a fixed service band for medium power satellite and the upper half of the KU-band (12.2 to 12.7 GHz) for high power direct broadcasting service (DBS). The KU-band is very powerful and does not require a large satellite dish; less than two feet in diameter is sufficient. Figure 7.3 illustrates KU-band communication satellites.

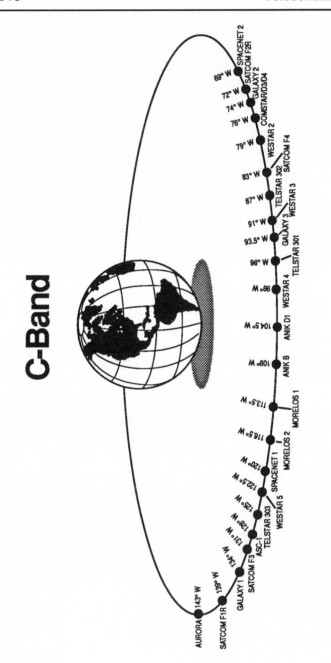

Figure 7.2. *C-Band communication satellites.*

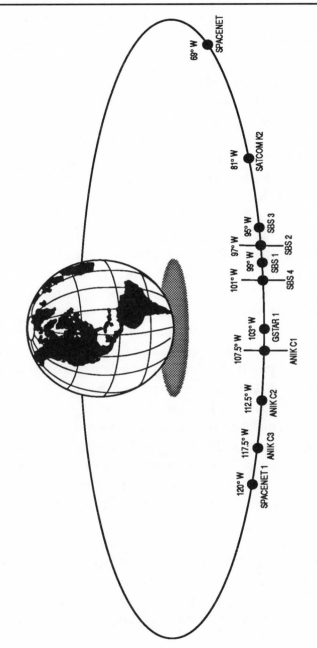

Figure 7.3. *KU-Band communication satellites.*

A New Solution for an Old Problem

Information is considered an organization's asset. The more information an institution possesses, the more accurate and efficient the decisions that will be made. Computer technology introduced society to the information revolution. Today's computer-powered information revolution is removing burdens of drudgery from the human brain, producing future gains in productivity, and bringing about significant changes in education, employment, competition, and social changes. (Sanders, p. 86, 1983).

Information accumulates at a phenomenal rate. Despite Arthur Clarke's opinion that the "world suffers from information starvation," the world is obsessed with information. The challenge is the access, distribution and delivery of information. Remote rural schools, for example, do not benefit from the availability of information as much as do schools in urban areas.

How could diversified programs be offered to these information-deprived areas? Are students in rural and urban areas exposed to the latest technology developments? Are there enough teachers to teach the various subjects? Are teachers conversant in new technology development? Is there coverage for teachers while they are in training? Is there any follow-up training for teachers? These questions and many more often remain unanswered. The resolutions may not be easily attained. Providing comprehensive, cost-effective training to cover both instructor and student in a convenient location seems to be complicated. On the contrary, the new technology offers a solution to an old problem.

Distance education is rather a new concept which brought great advantages to education, or more specifically, higher education. Aside from the financial problems, there are no limitations to using teleconferencing to enhance the quality of the teaching/learning process. "Telelearning" brings the participants together electronically, eliminating the need to travel to a central location. There is no difference between receiving a teleconference in one site or receiving more than one in different places. Practically, there would be no limitation on the number of participants, however, it might impose some restrictions on the process, especially interactive teleconferences.

A Tool for Learning

Teleconferencing has expanded the horizon of education. Attention is being directed to teleconferencing as a possible way of delivering instructional materials to students in a cost-effective way. The new technology presents information in a more concrete fashion and provides students with more accurate verbal and visual facsimiles. The speed and immediacy of information can be comprehended without special effort or skills.

Current applications of teleconferencing are already making it possible for educational institutions to include the home or office as a learning centers. Many studies have proven the validity of teleconferencing in the teaching/learning process. As an example, some of the studies will be examined here:

• The University of Missouri's Video Instructional Program aired a telecourse on adult basic education teaching methods via satellite nationwide. Analysis of the videotape lessons and audio teleconference found that participants talked 41 percent of the time and instructors 22 percent. Participants found the audio interaction made the course more productive (Henschke, 1991).

• A survey of the knowledge and attitudes of 485 California home economists toward the use of irradiation to preserve food revealed that they lacked the knowledge although they had a positive attitude toward it. An interactive teleconference on irradiation increased positive attitudes and improved knowledge (Johnson, 1990).

• A study compared the test scores of National Fire Academy (NFA) students who received on-campus classroom instruction and students who received the same instruction delivered by satellite teleconference. The results demonstrated no significant difference in test scores between on-campus students and teleconference students (Clark, 1989).

• A statewide interactive video teleconference was developed and presented to marketing educators, administrators, counselors, students, advisory committee members, and business people in Pennsylvania. The conference was designed to provide a technical update of the state of marketing in the United States as well as to unveil national strategies that can be implemented by marketing educators. The conference was rated very favorably by the participants (Palmieri, 1988).

• In an effort to broaden the context for classroom writing by providing an audience other than the teacher and classmates, a study used microcomputers, a modem, and an electronic mail service to set up communications with classes in other communities. Two classes at Sewickley Academy in Pennsylvania communicated for a semester with two classes from Wilsall, Montana and one class from Kyle, South Dakota. Students wrote in a variety of forms—notes, letters, stories, interviews, drafts, transcripts, and summaries. The three schools were extremely different from each other: Kyle is located on a Sioux reservation, Wilsall is a very small school in the Rocky Mountains, and Sewickley Academy is a private school in an affluent suburb of Pittsburgh. The students began their course investigating their preconceptions of the other communities, writing about and expressing their stereotypes freely in class. At the completion of the course, the majority of the Sewickley students agreed that they were more aware of cultural differences in the United States and had learned to question stereotypes, suggesting that the range of discourse was important not only in teaching students to be agile writers but also in providing a situation where students write to find out about different people and other communities. (Schwartz, 1987).

• A study was conducted of the use of a computer conferencing system developed by Participation Systems as enhancement for two independent study credit courses in the behavioral sciences, Introduction to Effective Communication and Introductory Psychology. Results of various evaluations of the computer conferencing indicate that the use of teleconferencing courses positively affects both the quality of the experience, and the attitudes and motivational levels of the students. Monitoring of the teleconferencing messages indicated that 90 percent of the students made substantial use of the system. The competition rates for the classes were comparable to the same courses taken in the traditional format, and better than the rates for the conventional independent study courses (Haile and Richards, 1984).

• Pennsylvania State University sponsored a telephone conference network experiment as a cost-effective format for providing inservice training in geriatric mental health for individuals who serve the elderly. The study showed that the majority of respondents reported high levels of satisfaction with the telephone conference network system and the specific program in which they participated and 85 percent reported that they would be able to use the skills learned in the program on the job. The convenience and efficiency of the telephone conference network were the most frequently mentioned strengths of the system (Connell and Smyer, 1984).

• A project was conducted to revise an existing office occupations curriculum to incorporate the use of telecommunications into simulated office practice and to train teachers in the use of equipment required to implement the updated curriculum.

Teachers from two high schools in the school district designed an office simulation system. A group of high school students were trained to use wordprocessing software to generate business documents and process them via telecommunictions through the various departments of a simulated business. Both the teachers and students who participated in the pilot testing of the curriculum found it to be a valuable learning experience (Burmester, 1984).

• An instructional program was developed and implemented at Kansas State University to provide career advancement training for respiratory therapy aides and technicians who have had on-the-job training in clinical experience in the basic respiratory therapy skills. The program was implemented under the auspices of TELENET, which is a teleconferencing delivery system based on the campus. The project staff concluded that the use of the TELENET delivery system enabled many individuals to receive training in respiratory therapy who would not otherwise have been able to receive it (Tinterow, 1984).

• Part of the North Slope Borough District, the two schools in the Inupiaq village of Wainwright, Alaska, began to take advantage of computer and audio-conference on the subject of using computers as communication tools. They began to use computers to communicate with supervisors in other locations, to teach math drills and practices, to teach science, and to improve research projects. However, the most interesting use of the computer was as a communications tool for instructional and administrative purposes. Using the computer and one of many electronic networks, students exchanged information with other students in California; teachers exchanged information with other teachers and with supervisors; administrators sent notes regarding travel schedules, book orders, test scores, and evaluation procedures; and university instructors presented information about the academic consequences of computers (Barnhardt, 1984).

Technological advancement has both facilitated and necessitated the development of teletraining. In developed countries, as Naylor states, distance education is often used to provide traditional education like that usually available in conventional institutions in the Western world. Whereas distance education in the Soviet Union focuses on improving productivity in the workplace, it is used in the United States to provide extension courses, adult basic education, regular postsecondary education programming, and professional continuing education (Naylor, 1985).

Instructional Use

New information technologies will raise the issues of how educational institutions should be restructured; how curricula should be changed and implemented; how teacher/faculty should be educated to keep pace with a rapidly changing, complex technological society; and what the roles of students and teaching personnel in the learning process should be. Rizzi remarks that institutions must prepare for high technology by having financial resources, expert personnel, equipment, instructional and faculty commitment, and short-range and long-range plans which are based on well-defined institutional needs, goals, objectives, and resources (Rizzi, 1984).

The applications of the teleconferencing in education could be used by students, teachers and administrators. Teleconferencing applications for students may be called instructional use and when used by teachers and administrators can be labeled in-service training or professional development. *Together they help students learn:*

— Teaching subjects (math, science, computer, etc.) in remote areas where experts are not available.
— Teaching new technology where access to the information is limited and costly.
— Teaching a subject in a big geographical area where standard instruction is crucial.
— Teaching materials in the multiple sites where the participants' interaction is desired.
— Teaching materials for great numbers of students where demonstration is critical.
— Teaching where a well-prepared presentation is necessary.
— Teaching a foreign language in multi-sites where a phone line is available.
— Teaching subject matters on different campuses where simultaneous instruction is desired.
— Teaching subject matter for adult education programs where attendance in class is a problem.
— Seeking experts' opinions on specific educational and social trends and issues when the experts are not physically nearby.
— Watching special academic events, such as speech, debate, or spelling contests.
— Listening to keynote speakers who cannot travel extensively and interaction is required.

In-Service Training or Professional Development

— Routine in-service training.
— Updating information.
— Immediacy of information.
— Timeliness of information.

— Inexpensive training for a large group.
— Renewing credentials.
— Multi-connection between different sites for interaction.
— Flexible hours, after school.
— Watching different models of teaching at different sites.
— Electronic visitation of facilities.
— Electronic class reunion.

In fact, many other applications can be added to the list but one very important point must be remembered: teleconferencing is not intended to replace the classroom teacher but, rather, to extend the classroom beyond the immediate walls.   Also, in applying this technology to instruction, caution should be employed because teleconferencing lacks the complexity of face-to-face instruction and interaction.   In addition, the sophistication level of equipment, in some cases, might be intimidating.   Although it may be easier for us to communicate with teleconferencing, it may also be easier for us to miscommunicate.

Hosting a Teleconference Successfully

Teleconferencing is a growing technology.   Every day thousands of students and professionals in the U. S. and around the world are linked electronically, sharing the latest developments in their own fields and interacting simultaneously with each other via phone lines or other means. Teleconferencing can occur between two locations (point to point) or between several different locations (point to multipoint).   The participants are encouraged to interact through a direct phone line.

Many educational and professional organizations are offering teleconferencing services and consultation. Among them are the Public Service Satellite Consortium (PSSC), established in 1975 to serve the telecommunications needs of non-profit organizations; the International Teleconferencing Association (ITCA), dedicated to advancing the teleconferencing profession; and the National University Teleconference Network (NUTN), one of the largest and fastest-growing networks of any kind, available to institutions of higher education. The latter has more than 170 member institutions in 37 states, the District of Columbia, and Canada.

With the initial investment of 700 to 2000 dollars, any school can purchase a satellite dish to bring teleconferencing programs into the building. In some instances, a rental mobile unit could be used. Inevitably, educational institutions will host an educational teleconferencing in the near future and students will electronically visit other students in the nation or around the world. An educator once said that teleconferencing will contribute to world peace if we connect the classrooms together around the globe and let students see themselves and communicate with each other.

Conducting a good teleconference adds to the effectiveness of the presentation. Hosting a teleconference successfully requires the host to consider certain simple steps and procedures. These steps and procedures can be broken down into three stages from the end-user point of view: before, during, and after teleconferencing.

Before Teleconferencing

The nature of teleconferencing calls for advance planning. The early announcement for a teleconference gives the end-user enough lead time to plan for the session carefully. Here are some suggestions:

At the beginning, a teleconference coordinator should be selected; this person could be from the faculty or an administrator. The general characteristics of the coordinator should include good planning ability, organization, communication, and decision-making skills.

Then, the coordinator should consider the following:

— Read the teleconference literature promptly. Normally the initial announcement defines objectives, procedures, and process of the teleconference. Make sure to read it carefully and make copies available for the interested group; also, post it on the bulletin board.

— Fill out the participation form, pay the required fee (if any) and mail it back. Sometimes registration by telephone is accepted.

— Know the satellite and the channel or transponder. If a fee is required, the transmitting satellite and receiving channel or transponder is not usually mentioned in the announcement. Upon receiving the payment, the satellite and the transponder will be released. Be certain to ask for the video and audio frequencies.

— Ask for the password in computer conferencing. In addition, the types of computer, modem, software, and printer should be identified.

— Check your facility for the given satellite and transponder. Some of the inexpensive satellite dishes are fixed and cannot be easily moved. Also, the satellite receiver could be dedicated to the specific satellite.

— Find a room of adequate size. The teleconference objective and target group should give you an idea of what size of room you need. Allow for a few extra seats in the back for late arrivals to minimize the distraction.

— Adjustable light control, from very dark to bright, is desirable.

— Provide a good-size television set for viewing the session. Viewers should be no further away than ten times the monitor size. For a 25-inch monitor, the maximum range would be 25 feet. The rule of thumb is no more than one person per diagonal inch of screen. A 25-inch monitor should serve no more than 25 people.

— Arrange for off-the-air taping if it is permitted. Many broadcasters grant permission to an institution to video-tape the teleconferencing for future reference.

— A telephone line and a telephone should be placed in the room. The telephone is needed for asking questions and it should be placed in the back of the room or, if possible, in a special booth to prevent audio feedback. In case of telephone conferencing, an amplifier is required.

— If you have participants from off campus, be sure to offer them directions and provide them with parking permits.

— Check your set-up on the day before. All arrangements and set-up should be in place the day before, if possible. This check gives you the assurance of working equipment.

— Call the originating site to confirm the date, time, satellite, and transponder. Some unforeseen technical problems might impose last minute changes.

— Arrive early. Allow yourself plenty of time in advance to recover from any last-minute, unexpected problems.

— Check the test signals. Half an hour before the teleconferencing, test signals will be transmitted. Check the video and audio signals for the optimum reception. In case of a problem, call the troubleshooting number which has already been given to the participating sites.

— Distribute handouts and the program's schedule. If the participants' reading ability is not at the handout level, read it for them.
— As facilitator, you might wish to make some introductory remarks regarding
  — teleconference objectives
  — the handling of questions and calling in
  — evaluation (if any)
— post-conference discussions and follow up (if any)
— parking, restrooms, and other housekeeping details

During Teleconferencing

— Check the equipment constantly. Try to be present in the room or have other staff available to place the calls and to be on hand to contact the technician in case of technical difficulty.
— Write the connecting phone number in a visible place.
— Ask the participants to write down their questions. For students in the lower grade levels, you should know exactly what they want to ask.
— Set up a priority for the questions. Students, particularly at the elementary or secondary levels tend to compete with each other in asking questions.
— Monitor dialing and phone conversation. Most of the time special instruction is given such as "do not call now" or "line is busy." Also, live broadcasts require careful use of language.
— Encourage students/participants to take notes. It is important that the highlights of the teleconference be remembered, comprehended, and discussed.
— Arrange for a light snack. Long teleconferencing has an intermission, which is a good time for serving food.

After Teleconferencing

— Distribute the evaluation form. If there is not a preexisting one you might want to develop one.

— Explain the evaluation form and the idea behind it. Young participants may need a little bit of help in understanding and filling out the form.

— Prepare students for the post-conference discussion. You may conduct a big-group discussions or several small group discussions.

— Ask students to write a report on the teleconferencing materials.

— Collect the evaluation forms. The majority of the teleconferencing originators want the participant's evaluation of the program.

— Thank the participants and inform them of possible follow up.

The above suggestions are guidelines. Not every school will need to implement every step; however, some may need to include even more steps to fit their needs. The teleconference coordinator may develop a checklist of the items he/she is supposed to do. Table 7. 1 suggests a checklist for the coordinator.

Table 7.1. Teleconference Coordinator's Checklist

BEFORE TELECONFERENCING:

—— Reading and distributing teleconference literature
—— Filling out participation form and mailing it back
—— Determining type of satellite and transponder
—— Determining the password, in case of computer conferencing
—— Checking the satellite dish and satellite receiver
—— Arranging a proper room
—— Providing a good-size TV set
—— Providing a phone line and a phone in the room
—— Checking the entire set-up on day before
—— Making the confirmation call to the originator
—— Arriving early on the teleconferencing day
—— Checking the test signals
—— Distributing the handouts and program schedule
—— Making introductory remarks and informing participants of
      the facilities

DURING TELECONFERENCING:

—— Checking the equipment and troubleshooting
—— Making calling-in number available
—— Helping students in asking questions
—— Providing snack

AFTER TELECONFERENCING:

—— Evaluating the program
—— Participating in a group discussion
—— Making the closing remarks

References

Azarmsa, Reza. (1987). Teleconferencing: An Instructional Tool. *Educational Technology*. December, 28-32.

Azarmsa, Reza. (1987). Teleconferencing: How to Be a Successful Host. *TechTrends*. September, 19-23.

Barnhardt, Carol. (1984). *"Let Your Fingers Do the Talking" : Computer Communication in an Alaskan Rural School.* (ERIC Document Reproduction Service No. ED241 242).

Bjorklund, Jan and Fredmeyer, Joanne. (1985). Keeping Current Via Teleconferencing. *Journal of Extension*, Summer, 21-24.

Burmester, Allen. (1984). *Telecommunications. Final Report.* November. (ERIC Document Reproduction Service No. ED255 679).

Clark, Burton. (1989). *Comparison of Achievement of Students in On-Campus Classroom Instruction versus Satellite Teleconference Instruction.* (ERIC Document Reproduction Service No. ED327668).

Connell, C. and Smyer, M. A. (1984). *Training in Mental Health: Evaluation of the Telephone Conference Network.* November. (ERIC Document Reproduction Service No. ED255 780).

Cowan, Robert. (1984). *Teleconferencing Maximizing Human Potential.* Reston, Virginia: Reston Publishing Co., Inc.

Eastman, Susan Tyler. (1985). Teleconferencing in Education and Business. *Feedback*, Summer,8-11.

Easton, Anthony T. (1983). *The Satellite TV Handbook.* Indianapolis, IN: Howard W. Sams & Co., Inc.

Haile, Penelope J. and Richards, Angela J. (1984). *Supporting the Distance Learner with Computer Teleconferencing.* October. (ERIC Document Reproduction Service No. ED256 293).

Henschke, John. (1991). Innovating with Telecommunications. *Adult Learning*, January, 9-10.

Johanson, Robert. (1984). *Teleconferencing and Beyond.* New York: Mc Graw-Hill.

Johnson, Fay. (1990). Knowledge and Attitudes of Selected Home Economists toward Irradiation in Food Preservation. *Home Economics Research Journal*, December, 170-183.

Kurland, Norman D. (1983). Have Computer, Will Not Travel: Meeting Electronically. *Phi Delta Kappan*, October, 122+.

Nayler, Michele. (1985). *Distance Education. Overview.* (ERIC Document Reproduction Service No. ED259 214).

Olson, David. (1985). Satellite Session for Major Meetings. *E-ITV Magazine*, November, 30-31.

Palmieri, Frank. (1988). *Marketing Education Teleconference. Final Report.* (ERIC Document Reproduction Service No. ED326723).

Portway, Patrick. (1984). What Teleconferencing Adds, Not Eliminates. *Office*, April, 101+.

Ratcliff, James L. (1985). Statewide Teleconference Educational Programming: Strategic Planning Issues. *Catalyst*, Volume XIV, Number 1, 12-16.

Rizzi, Rose A. (1984). *Impact and Implications of Technological Change on Educational Institutions.* (ERIC Document Reproduction Service No. ED249 944).

Rogan, Randall G. and Simmons, Gary A. (1984). Teleconferencing. *Journal of Extension*, September/October, 27-31.

Sanders, Donald. (1983). *Computers Today.* New York: McGraw-Hill.

Schwartz, Jeffrey. (1987). *Using an Electronic Network To Create a Read Context for High School Writing.* (ERIC Document Reproduction Service No. ED291105).

Standard & Poor's. (1991). *Industry Survey*. Vol. 2. New York: Standard & Poor's Corporation.

_____ (1986). Telecom VI-World's Largest Teleconferencing Show. *Teleconference,* September/October, 10-11.

Thiel, Carol T. (1984). Teleconferencing—A New Medium for Your Message. *InfoSystems*, April, 64-68.

_____ (1985). Turn on to Ku-Band. *Satellite Orbit,* December, 38+.

Tyson, John. (1985). Satellite Sessions for Decision-Making. *E-ITV Magazine*, November, 27-29.

U.S. Department of Commerce. (1991). *U.S. Industrial Outlook, 1991*. Washington, DC: US Government Printing Office.

U.S. Bureau of Economic Analysis. (1984). *The Detailed Input-Output Structure of the U. S. Economy*. Washington, DC: US Government Printing Office.

_____ (1985). *Videoconference Primer*. San Jose, CA: Compression Labs, Inc.

Winn, Bill et al. (1986). The Design and Application of a Distance Education System Using Teleconferencing and Computer Graphics. *Educational Technology*, January, 19-23.

Chapter Eight

Distance Learning

Introduction

The concept of distance learning is not new in the delivery of education. For years, institutions have relied on remote education. Before television, students took correspondence courses and listened to instructional radio. Once television entered our homes in great numbers in the '50s, video instruction entered our homes as well, from educational television stations that started to spring up across the country. VCRs changed the concept of distance learning, too, giving learners the opportunity to take classes at their convenience. Computers and data communications have stimulated universal interest in the area of distance learning: the live transmission of instruction from teachers located at one or more distant locations. Courses not otherwise locally available or affordable are being provided to educational institutions with small numbers of students.

What Is Distance Learning?

Distance learning usually refers to a situation where the learner and the educator use telecommunications or electronic devices (cable, satellite, fiber optics, broadcast, video, and computer technology) to *interactively* follow part or all of a course program.

The U. S. Department of Education's Office of Educational Research and Improvement defines distance learning as: "The application of telecommunications and electronic devices which enables students and learners to receive instruction that originates from some distant location. Typically, the learner is given the capacity to interact with the instructor or program directly, and given the opportunity to meet with the instructor on a periodic basis." As the definition implies, the key issue in the process of distance learning is that distance learning involves some electronic devices and enables students to learn from instruction that originates someplace else. The difference between this and an open university telecourse or educational television, is that this is interactive, two-way technology.

Distance learning, or distance education, has evolved slowly, from correspondence courses to interactive computer-mediated telecommunications and the evolution of distance learning will continue for some time.

The distinction between distance and traditional learners is often more societal. The distance learner may include the following groups:

— The geographically disadvantaged.
— The physically disabled.
— The financially disadvantaged (because it is cheaper than building a school).

— Those simply wanting to take advantage of the opportunities electronic media provides.
— Those in need of remediation.
— Those who want to avoid particular learning dynamics or particular content.
— Those wanting to protect cultural lifestyle and mobility.

Distance learning provides equity of educational opportunity and makes up for the lack of conventional resources (Bruder, 1989). The advantages of distance learning include the following:

— Offsets time and distance constraints in the delivery and utilization of educational services.
— Provides educational services to those unable to participate in conventional learning.
— Provides continuing education to adults who wish to acquire new skills and knowledge.
— Adapts to student's lifestyle.
— Allows both individualized and mass education.
— Makes up for the lack of conventional resources.
— Integrates into the community through use of local resources.

What Do Researchers Say?

A 1989 report from the federal Office of Technology Assessment, titled *Linking for Learning: A New Course for Education*, reviewed distance learning on the national level, and offered these findings:

• Distance learning is changing educational boundaries that have traditionally been defined by location and by institution. Using distance learning technology, classrooms can now extend to students in other schools, in other cities, in other states, and in other nations. A high school course in advanced mathematics may be taught by a university professor in a live, interactive situation linking high school students in inner-city areas of Los Angeles, Boston, Detroit, and rural areas of California.

• On the K-12 level, providing educational services for the geographically isolated schools and for underserved or advanced students has been the principal application of distance learning. More recently, it is being viewed as a means of solving other educational deficiencies, including inadequacies in faculty and staff development, parental involvement, and cultural relations.

• The recent expansion of distance learning has provided a unique opportunity for collaboration and resource sharing by educators from various institutional, instructional, and geographic locations. Joint activities by representatives from public schools, higher education, and the private sector, have multiplied significantly during the past five years, seeking to use distance learning as a means to respond to the need for improved educational services.

• There is no single best model of distance learning. The technology is flexible and offers multiple ways to deliver instruction over a distance. The quality and effectiveness of distance learning are determined by the quality of the educational program being transmitted and the selection of the appropriate technologies to transmit the instruction.

• Research on the effectiveness of distance learning has consistently concluded that, when used in business, military training, and adult learning, no significant difference exists in effectiveness between traditional instruction methods and distance learning (Moore, 1989). Student attitudes are generally positive. While favorable anecdotal evidence has been gathered, the research on distance learning in the K-12 setting is not conclusive, as few long-term evaluations have been conducted.

National Distance Learning Projects

Federal support for comprehensive distance learning projects has been provided through the Star Schools Program, established in 1987 to address "two critical needs in the rebuilding of our educational system to meet domestic and international challenges. The nation's students must have access to basic and advanced courses in mathematics, science, and foreign languages, and these courses must be of the highest quality" (U. S. Senate Committee on Labor and Human Resources, 1987, page 1). The program is designed to create multistate partnerships to write and deliver both core and enrichment curriculum and to provide instruction for disadvantaged students. The program is authorized for a five-year period, with a funding limit of $100 million.

The first round of two-year grants went to four projects: (1) Satellite Educational Resources Consortium (SERC); (2) TI-IN United Star Network; (3) the Midlands Consortium; and (4) Technical Education Research Centers (TERC).

The second round of Star School Grants was announced recently by the U.S. Department of Education, with $14.8 million awarded to four new partnerships:

• Telecommunications Education for Advances in Mathematics and Science Education (TEAMS) will be directed by the Los Angeles County Office of Education and include four public school districts—Los Angeles, Washington, D.C., Detroit, and Boston. With $3,450,000 in funding, the project will develop programs dealing with multicultural mathematics, problem solving in grades 7-10, science and technology experiences for grades 4-5, student-to-student teleconferences in grades 7-12, and career exploration for grades 7-12 in mathematics and science.

• The Pacific Northwest Educational Telecommunications Partnership will provide education to students in Alaska, Idaho, Montana, Oregon, and Washington, as well as in the Pacific Rim Territories. With $5,050,000 in funding for 1990-91, the project will emphasize the provision of science, mathematics, Japanese and other foreign language instruction to low-income and migrant students.

• Central Education Telecommunications Consortium will be administered by the Black College Satellite Network (BCSN). Working partnerships will be developed between historically Black colleges, the District of Columbia school district, and other predominantly Black school districts. With a grant of $1,400,000, teachers will receive training in science and mathematics instruction, as well as in the Chinese, Swahili, and Arabic languages.

• "Reach for the Stars" is directed by the Massachusetts Corporation for Educational Telecommunication (MCET) with 20 participating organizations including four state departments of education. The $4,913,000 grant will be used to develop science experiences for middle school students and will focus on community-wide science resources such as museums.

A second major source of funding for national distance learning projects is the Annenberg/CPB Project, which provided $1.8 to seven projects under its new three-year initiative, "New Pathways to a Degree: Using Technologies to Open the College." The seven new projects will include 27 colleges and universities in Indiana, Maine, Minnesota, New York, Oregon, Virginia, and West Virginia, and they will serve approximately 10,000 students in 1993. The seven projects are:

• The Oregon State System of Higher Education will develop a model for how colleges can offer complete baccalaureate degree programs via Oregon Ed-Net, the statewide educational network.

Participating institutions will offer undergraduate programs in agricultural business management, liberal studies, and nursing. Ed-Net will connect hundreds of public schools, libraries, and colleges using satellite, two-way audio and video communications, fiber optics, and computers. Innovative ways for providing special student services will be developed.

• Indiana University/Purdue University at Indianapolis (IUPUI) is developing a model for how urban universities can provide access and community support for minority students. IUPUI will focus on core liberal arts courses and will use cable television, networked computers and facsimile machines to reach students at local community and education centers, churches, and a vocational technical college.

• The University of Maine at Augusta, on behalf of the Community College of Maine, will build on its current system that links all public higher education institutions with off-campus sites. The university will offer a coherent sequence of courses for an Associate of Arts degree and an Associate of Science degree, utilizing videodiscs, computer instruction, and computer conferencing to enrich the curriculum. The associate degree will be accepted for transfer to four-year programs at all public universities in Maine. A model training program for faculty, student support staff, and technical staff also will be implemented.

• The College of St. Catherine in St. Paul is serving as a model for how colleges — particularly those that offer weekend degree programs — can use technology to remove educational barriers and meet the needs of the adult student with career and family responsibilities. Electronic mail, computer conferencing, video and audiocassettes, and facsimile machines will link students in their homes, businesses, or through nearby libraries, campuses, or other community facilities. Core liberal studies courses and some upper-division courses toward the Information Management degree will be offered.

• Rochester Institute of Technology in Rochester, New York, is developing an affordable model for using technology to offer highly accessible upperdivision courses. The program will use interactive technologies, such as audiographic and computer conferencing, picture phones, and on-line library services to develop 40 upper-division courses from which students can structure degree programs in applied arts and sciences. The campus will be linked electronically to remote sites 100 or more miles from the campus, and the courses will use videotaped lectures to allow students to choose where and when they study.

• Northern Virginia Community College in Annandale, Virginia, will use public television, cable, computer conferencing, two-way compressed video, audio conferencing, voice mail, and videocassettes to offer complete associate degrees in General Studies and Business Administration. The degrees are intended for students who plan to pursue a baccalaureate degree at a four-year institution.

• West Virginia University in Morgantown will work with a statewide coalition to offer general studies and business management courses to rural adults. In cooperation with West Virginia's higher education system, educational broadcasting authority, library commission, and satellite delivery network, the University will use satellite video, facsimile, and electronic mail to serve rural learners in their homes, at the 16 public higher education institutions, and in public libraries, public schools, businesses, and county extension offices.

A new national project has been initiated by Hughes Aircraft, designed to use satellite technology to improve the quality of America's elementary education. The "Galaxy Classroom" is being planned to offer interactive mathematics, science, English, and language arts instruction to K-5 students in urban and rural locations in various parts of the country. The objective of the program is to "improve academic achievement among children who come from diverse backgrounds, to promote educational excellence by developing sound content, and to motivate children by promoting an enjoyment of learning, self-esteem, and responsibility" (Hezel, 1991, p. 1). The Galaxy Classroom will begin to provide instruction in 1993.

• Mississippi 2000 is two-way video and audio interactive distance learning. It offers a prototype for schools within the state and around the country—in both rural settings and in the inner city. It is a unique network of corporate partners, of teachers and students, and of technology—all working with the state of Mississippi. Four high schools in Clarksdale, Corinth, Philadelphia and West Point are connected on the Mississippi 2000 network via 11,000 miles of fiber optics. In addition, the Mississippi Educational Television Network, Mississippi State University and the Mississippi University for Women are also connected to the network. The Mississippi School for Math and Science participates by providing instructors for some of the courses.

Through a unique partnership of five corporate leaders and the state of Mississippi, Mississippi 2000 represents a union of technology and telecommunications with the resources of superior teachers. Each of the five corporate partners (South Central Bell, Northern Telecom, IBM Corporation, ADC Telecommunications, and Apple Computer) contributed time, technology and expertise to create this network (Mabus, 1991).

California Distance Learning Projects: Some of the most important distance learning projects operating in California are:

• The Los Angeles County Office of Education has established, during the past two years, the Educational Telecommunications Network (ETN), utilizing satellite technology to telecast live, interactive staff development to school districts in 35 counties in California.

• The Los Angeles Unified School District operates a broadcast television station—KLCS—including a "Homework Hotline" allowing students to receive on-air tutoring after school.

• California State University, Chico (CSUC), offers regular university courses, including a master's degree program in computer science, by televised instruction by satellite to students in 15 states. CSUC also offers programming for K-12 students and teachers, including a first-year teacher training program called "Partners."

• California State University, Sacramento (CSUS), has established a computer-based Learning Solutions Network (LSN) that currently reaches 4,500 students at 30 public schools in California. The program targets current and potential high school dropouts, offering courses in basic reading, mathematics, study skills, critical thinking, and typing. The course work is developed by the University of Illinois in Urbana. The satellite dishes of CSUS capture the coursework, and the secondary schools use their computers and telephone lines to access the information that CSUS retrieves.

• California State University, Bakersfield (CSUB), has established a pilot program with Tehachapi High School using compressed video over a high capacity telephone linkage cable to transmit two-way video between the campus and students and teachers at the rural school. In addition to compressed video, CSUB uses ITFS, cable, and microwave relay to offer courses to different areas. Through its Young Scholar Program, CSUB offers college credit courses to high school students at more than 17 designated sites for $2.00. Figure 8.1 illustrates the distance learning region for CSUB.

• Several State University campuses offer university credit courses to advanced high school students as well as college students, using satellite and microwave technology. For example, California State Polytechnic University, Pomona, offers live televised university courses to high school students in 245 schools in the Los Angeles area. The California State University system has a microwave network connecting four of its campuses in northern and central California, with the system managed from its Chico campus.

• Forty-two southern California colleges, representing 26 community college districts, have established a consortium to develop, distribute, and acquire college credit telecommunications-based instructional materials. More than 27,000 students enrolled in consortium courses during the 1989-90 academic year, with each course typically including an integrated learning package consisting of 26 video lessons, a textbook, study guide, exam bank, faculty manual, and an on-campus instructor. The courses are distributed through a multi-faceted network, including Public Broadcasting (PBS) and commercial television stations, cable, ITFS, and satellite systems.

• Stanford University has been a national pioneer in the use of telecommunications for off-campus delivery of engineering programs. It uses microwave and ITFS systems in the Bay Area and satellite distribution to reach sites throughout the country.

Figure 8.1. *Distance learning region at California State University, Bakersfield.*

Distance Learning Delivery Systems

There are many public and private institutions and agencies using video communications for instruction within formal and nonformal education settings. The major instructional delivery systems are noncommercial broadcasting, closed-circuit TV, cable systems, instructional television fixed services (ITFS), satellite transmission, video instruction, and compressed technology.

Noncommercial Broadcasting

The 290-plus TV stations in the United States that hold noncommercial licenses are referred to collectively as public television stations, a term designating their common commitment to operate not for private gain but for public benefit. Although these stations have various patterns of ownership, they tend to operate along roughly similar lines. Just as most commercial stations act as outlets for commercial network programming, most public television stations serve as outlets for the network programming of the Public Broadcasting Service (PBS). Their evening schedules feature PBS offerings and other programs aimed at home viewers in general, while during the daytime hours these stations typically carry instructional programs.

Public television attempts to offer an alternative type of programming for viewers that are not well served by the mass audience programs of commercial broadcasting. In reaching out to selected subgroups, public TV programming does not usually attract viewers on a scale comparable to the commercial networks. However, well-produced programs have won critical acclaim and loyal audiences that in recent years have grown to a size comparable to those of their commercial rivals.

As mentioned above in regard to commercial programs, the types of programs carried on public TV—documentaries, dramas, public affairs features, musical performances, science programs and the like—are often useful as adjuncts to instruction.

Instructional Programming

Programs for direct classroom use are a mainstay of most public TV stations' daytime schedules. The average transmits about 40 elementary and 20 secondary series. There is also a rapidly growing trend toward distribution of programs by stations.

In 1981 PBS launched the Adult Learning Services (ALS) as a major initiative to make college courses and other learning experiences available to adult learners everywhere. In the years since, millions of students have taken ALS telecourses offered by more than 1800 colleges and universities in conjunction with the nation's public television stations.

In 1988, ALS addressed the growing demand from colleges and businesses for new and more diverse educational programming by launching the Adult Learning Satellite Service (ALSS). Through ALSS and its business-oriented programming strand, The Business Channel, colleges with satellite receiver equipment now have direct access to telecourse, resource programming, and live, interactive videoconferences.

By expanding access to college-level education, telecourses benefit students, faculty, and colleges. Students earn college credit, learn proficiencies for the work world, and improve the quality of their lives through enriched learning experiences. Faculty use an effective instructional resource, gain professional expertise, and assist a new student population. Colleges and universities offer students a convenient and flexible alternative to traditional classroom instruction, enrich their curricula, and reach out to new students. ITV programs are often repeated at different hours throughout the week to allow for flexibility in classroom scheduling. Broadcast ITV programs usually do not present core instruction in basic subject areas. The ITV roles in instruction are:

— To assist the classroom teachers in those subjects in which they often have the most difficulty (for example, art, music, "new" mathematics, science, and health).
— To supplement the classroom instruction in subject areas in which limited classroom resources may prevent full examination of historical or international events.
— To bring outside stimulation in subject areas, such as literature, where teachers have difficulty exciting and motivating the students.

Closed-Circuit Television

The term closed-circuit television refers to a TV distribution system in which the sender and receiver are physically linked by wire. At its simplest, a connection between a single camera and a receiver within the same room (e.g. for image magnification in a science lab) constitutes closed-circuit TV (CCTV). Or several classrooms could be linked to a studio to form a building-wide CCTV system. Campus-wide and school-district-wide interconnections are also possible. In some areas, one finds campus and district centers connected by statewide CCTV linkages forming networks of impressive scope. For special purposes, transcontinental telephone lines can be leased to set up CCTV hookups of national scope. A common example is the showing of championship boxing matches in theaters projected on a large screen.

Another application is the videoconference, a teleconference business meeting in which the participants can see each other as they converse. This special closed-circuit application requires elaborate technical arrangements to work well.

One of the principal advantages of CCTV is that such systems, since they do not operate through the airwaves controlled by government agencies, can be set up freely by anyone who has the money to do so. Although the cost tends to increase with the size of the coverage area (unlike through-the-air delivery systems), the freedom, privacy, and multichannel capability of CCTV makes it an attractive option for some educational purposes.

Because cost increases as geographic coverage increases, CCTV is not widely used in large school districts. It has, however, become the leading delivery system for ITV on college and university campuses.

Cable Television

The cable concept of television program delivery was first applied commercially in the 1950s in isolated towns where, due to interference from a mountain overshadowing the town, people were unable to receive a viewable signal from the nearest TV station. Local businessmen developed the idea of building a master antenna atop the mountain. There the weak signals were amplified and fed into a coaxial cable that ran down the mountain into the town. By paying an installation charge and a monthly subscription fee, a customer could have his or her home connected to the cable. This idea of having a single tall antenna to serve a whole community gave the process the name community antenna television, or CATV, now more commonly known as cable television.

Most CATV systems in operation today still basically resemble the original master antenna model. The signals are amplified and delivered to the head-end of the system where they are processed, fed into a trunk line, and further amplified. The signals then proceed along feeder lines and that enter individual homes and other buildings.

The cable subscriber, besides getting a strong, clear video image on the screen, has access to more channels than are readily available over the air. Some of these channels are "public access" outlets for use by community and special interest groups. Others are used for sporting events, special movie showings, programs imported from distant independent stations, etc.

Thousands of educational institutions are now plugged into CATV system, often without charge from the local cable operator. In many cases, schools and colleges are operating public access channels for their own institutional and/or instructional purposes.

The availability of multiple channels facilitates a number of special services: (1) transmission of several programs at different hours for more flexible matching with classroom schedules; (2) the aiming of specialized programs at small subgroups, for example, those speaking foreign languages or having sight or hearing impairment; (3) retrieval of remotely stored libraries of video materials, allowing teachers—or individual students— access to materials on demand without the logistic struggle often associated with instructional media use.

Actually, the number of channels available on many cable systems is still small, the average system supplying less than a dozen channels. Recent developments, however (such as fiber optics as a replacement for coaxial cable and improvements in the system's other hardware components), foreshadow the development of CATV systems capable of supporting scores, even hundreds, of transmission channels.

But what has caused futurists among educators to really sit up and take notice is the characteristic of CATV which most distinguishes it from other television delivery systems: its ability to transmit signals not only from sender to receiver but also from the receiver back to sender. Although most cable systems today send signals only "down-stream" to the home or school, the technology is available to permit return communications "up-stream" back to the sender. These return signals can take the form of simple yes/no digital communications, audio signals alone, or full television images with accompanying sound. Each of these feedback possibilities evokes exciting prospects for converting ITV into a two-way, interactive medium of instructional communication.

Instructional Television Fixed Service (ITFS)

In 1963, eleven years after the Federal Communications Commission reserved certain VHF (Very High Frequency) and UHF (Ultra High Frequency) channels for noncommercial use, it established the Instructional Television Fixed Service (ITFS), setting aside channels in the microwave band of 2500-2690 MHz for instructional use by educational institutions. Later rules allowed the ITFS to expand into the areas of audio and hard-copy transmission and into two-way television systems.

The ITFS system has one major technical limitation. Signals broadcast at these high microwave frequencies travel in a line-of-sight pattern. Consequently, coverage of ITFS is limited to areas in direct sightline of the transmission tower.

Nevertheless, this coverage is sufficient in many educational situations. Coverage can generally extend over areas about the size of a large school district, and, unlike closed-circuit television, no wiring is required for connection among classrooms. Like cable, ITFS allows transmission on multiple channels; the average licensee operates about six channels. This greatly expands the broadcasting possibilities in a given locale beyond what would exist merely with VHF and UHF outlets. Because the system operates on frequencies above those that can be received on ordinary sets without a converter, it offers a higher degree of audience selectivity and programming privacy than regular broadcast television.

Within higher education, ITFS, in addition to offering college credit courses to high school students, is used predominantly for graduate and professional school extension purposes.

In short, ITFS is a delivery system with considerable potential. It may well come to play a more prominent role in the future as the available frequencies in the VHF and UHF bands become saturated and educators seek additional channels for distributing video materials. Figure 8.2 lists the important components of the ITFS system.

Satellite: Direct Home Reception

Communication satellites now carry most international telephone calls as well as most broadcast telephone transmissions. Virtually all of today's satellites are placed in a geosynchronous orbit—an orbit synchronized with the speed of the earth's own rotation. By keeping pace with the spin of the earth, they appear to remain motionless above the same spot on the ground. Geosynchronous satellites operate as transmitting stations on top of an imaginary tower so tall (22,300 miles high) that they can "see" nearly half of the earth's surface at one time. Theoretically, three properly placed geosynchronous satellites could cover the entire

CONTROL ROOM EQUIPMENT

Video Patch Panal
Audio Patch Panal
FrameSync/Router w/Rackit
Aural Exciter/Comp/Limiter
Active Combining Card
Automatic Mic Mixer/Combiner
16mm Projector Video Converter
35mm Projector Video Converter
Time Base Corrector
Video Switcher
Digital Border Generator
Speakers
S-VHS Video Recorder/Player
Triple Monitors
Character Generator
Wireless Mic Transmitter/Receiver
Sync/Test Generator
Power Supply Module
Video DA
Audio DA
U-Matic SP Video Player
Power Amp
Telephone Hybird
Mic Mixer
Audio Cassette Deck
Pan-Tilt-Zoom-Focus Remote
Video Routing Switcher
Demodulator

CLASSROOM EQUIPMENT

2/3" CCD Camera Lens
Boundary Mic
Data Saver Electronic board
CCD Video Camera/WV-F300
Remote Control Unit
Tripods
35" Color Monitor
5/8 Wave Antenna
Lav Mic
Acoustic Wall Cover
Classroom Furniture

TRANSMITTER/STL-LINK

ITFS Transmit Antennae
Connecting Componets
10-Watt Transmitter
4-Channel Combiner
Remote Panel & Meter
Switching System
50-Watt Transmitter
Fiber Optic Cable
Connector Panel

OFFICE EQUIPMENT & SUPPORT

Computers
Software (Word Processing, Database,
  Spreadsheet, Page layout, Graphics)
Laser Printer
Typewriter
Two Page Display Monitor w/Gray
  Scale Card
Memory-Backup Device
Modem
File Cabinets
Office Furniture

RECEIVE SITE EQUIPMENT

Grid Dish with mounting pipe
ITFS Receivers
5" Color Monitor
Antenna Tripod
Cable
60' Self Support Tower
Processor
Hetrodyne Unit
IF Unit
Converter Unit
ITFS Receivers
Antenna Mounting Brackets

Figure 8.2. *Major components of ITFS system*

globe. However, because of the immense and growing amount of communications traffic, over 80 satellites are actually in use at this time.

Private individuals and organizations have already begun setting up their own backyard dish antennas, sometimes referred to as TVRO's, for "Television Reception Only." By aiming a TVRO at one of the dozen satellites hovering over North America you can tap directly into the nonstop stream of television programming that is constantly being relayed by American and Canadian broadcasters and cable operators. The richness of the resource is indisputable: commercial and educational programs, sports, movies, special ethnic programming, and more.

Video Instruction

The final delivery system involves neither wires nor over-the-air broadcasting. We are using the term video instruction to refer to the several methods of playing back ITV programs right in the classroom by means of video recorders. The distribution system itself—the record/playback machine—is portable and can be set up wherever needed.

References

California Postsecondary Education Commission. (1991). *State Policy on Technology for Distance Learning.* Commission Report 91-7, April.

California State University Commission on Instructional Technology. (1990). *The Student, The Faculty, and the Information Age: The Power of Technology.* Long Beach: Office of the Chancellor, The California State University, January.

California Technology Project. (1990). *Distance Learning for California School's Task Force Recommendations.* Seal Beach: California Technology Project.

California Technology Project and the Regional Educational Television Advisory Council. (1990). *California Distance Learning Summit Report.* Downey: The Council.

California Technology Project Distance Learning Task Force. (1990). *Distance Learning for California Schools: A Resource Guide on Live Interactive Televised Instruction.* Seal Beach: California Technology Project.

Clark, Thomas A. and Verdiun, John R., Jr. (1989). Distance Education: Its Effectiveness and Potential Use in Lifelong Learning. *Lifelong Learning*, January.

Dively, Dwight. (1991). *State Planning and Implementation of Educational Telecommunications in the West.* Boulder, CO: Western Cooperative for Educational Telecommunications.

Ellertson, Kent. (1987). *Report on Distance Learning: A National Effectiveness Survey.* Mansfield University, Pennsylvania: Pennsylvania Teleteaching Project.

Hezel Associates. (1991). *Statewide Planning for Telecommunications in Education.* Washington, D.C.: The Annenberg/ Corporation for Public Broadcasting Project.

Hobbs, Vicki M., and Osburn, Donald D. (1989). *Distance Learning Evaluation Study Report: An Inter- and Intra-State Comparison. A Study of North Dakota and Missouri Schools Implementing German I by Satellite.* Stillwater: Oklahoma State University.

Jonsen, Richard W., and Johnstone, Sally. (1991). The Future of Information Technology in Higher Education—The State Perspective. *Change,* January/February, 42-46.

Lienau, Larry. (1987). *Evaluation of Teaching/Learning at a Distance.* Proceeding: Third Annual Conference on Teaching at a Distance. Madison, Wisconsin. August.

Mabus, Ray (1991). A New Light in Education: Mississippi 2000. *T. H. E. Journal,* August, 52-56.

Moore, Michael. (1989). *Effects of Distance Learning: A Summary of the Literature.* Office of Technology Assessment Contractor Report, May.

Taylor, Daniel, Sanford, Clarke, and Brynjulson, Barry. (1990). An Electronic Network for Distance Learning: CSU Bakersfield and Terrestrial Telephone Lines. *Teleconference,* September, 34-36.

U.S. Congress, Office of Technology Assessment. (1989). *Linking for Learning: A New Course for Education.* Washington, D. C.: U.S. Government Printing Office, November.

Ward, Jaci. (1990). Landline Two-Way Video: Being Three—And Here. *T. H. E. Journal,* May, 59-61.

Western Cooperative for Educational Telecommunications. (1990). *Communique.* Boulder, CO: Western Interstate Commission for Higher Education, November.

Chapter Nine

Designing a
Network System

Introduction

Network design exemplifies the more general systems analysis and design process used to design any computer-based system. Computer systems analysis and design together form a much newer discipline. While the process is becoming more scientific with each passing year, there are still many aspects that are somewhat "artistic" in nature. The methods and techniques are gradually becoming standardized as people in industry gain experience and understand the process and the work required.

Network design is a process for understanding the requirements for a communications network, investigating alternative ways for implementing the network, and selecting the most appropriate alternative to provide the required capability. The work is performed by a project team that has the responsibility to analyze the requirements, design the new network, and implement it.

In every network design, certain work must be performed, much of it in a particular sequence. That is why network design is normally broken into steps that are completed in sequence. The steps are called by various names in different organizations, and the dividing lines between steps vary a little from region to region. Overall, however, every network design requires the same general work. The goal of the network design process is to ensure that the network satisfies user requirements at an appropriate cost.

Several steps should be used when designing a new communication network. The following contains a list and detailed descriptions of each of the recommended steps.

Conducting a Feasibility Study

Possibly, this step may already have been performed by the school administrators who have identified the problem, the purpose, and the objectives of the proposed system.

A primary responsibility in proceeding with a feasibility study is to define the problem clearly and to put it in writing. Problem definition involves identifying all the issues that may indicate the need for a data communication network. Any of the following needs assessment factors may be analyzed to determine if the school needs this new network:

— Increased volume of inputs/outputs.
— Inadequate data processing.
— Obsolete hardware/software.
— Inadequate file structures (database).
— Unsatisfactory movement of data/information throughout the school/district.
— Inadequate interfacing between application systems and other staff.
— Untimely availability of documentation.
— Unreliability of current systems.
— Inability to maintain current systems.
— Inadequate security/privacy.

— Decreasing productivity.
— Inadequate training.
— Future growth that requires new methods.
— Negative effect of old system on teachers' and administrators' morale.
— Inadequate floor space for personnel/files.
— Avoidance of future costs.
— Need for more timely access to information for improved decision-making.
— Increasing flow of information/paperwork.
— Need to expand capacity for access to instructional materials.
— Need to increase level of instructional quality.
— Need for new methods and better exchange of information in connecting at national and international levels.
— Reduction of inventories.
— Need for a paperless office.
— Desire to take advantage of using future technology in the educational environment.

Once the problem has been defined according to these factors, the purpose and objectives of the new data communication network are identified, the scope or boundaries the system will encompass are established, and perhaps some preliminary "magnitudes" of cost can be identified.

The feasibility study might include some preliminary work on the geographical scope of the network. The feasibility study results might also be presented verbally. This type of presentation provides school board members and school administrators with an opportunity to ask questions or discuss issues that may have a bearing on whether to proceed.

Preparing a Plan

At this point, the feasibility study has been completed, and the school administrator has given its approval to proceed with the design and development of a data communication network.

While beginning a new design, develop some *evaluation criteria*. If such criteria are developed at the beginning, then there is a yardstick at completion for measuring the success of the data communication network or system design, development, and implementation. The following *evaluation criteria* should be considered and should be given a numerical value at the beginning of the project. This value is used to provide the means of comparison that management needs to evaluate the project properly.

The following evaluation criteria can be used to evaluate the new data communication network after it has been developed.

Time: Are elapsed time, transaction time, overall processing time, response time, or other operational times reduced?

Cost: Are annual system cost, per unit cost, and maintenance, operational, investment, and implementation costs reduced?

Quality: Is a better product or service being produced? Is there less repetitive work because of the system? Has the quality of data and information improved? How can these quality factors be measured?

Capacity: Does the system have the capacity to handle workloads, peak loads, and average loads, as well as the long-term future capacity to meet the school's needs in the next decade?

Efficiency: Is the system more efficient than the previous one?

Productivity: Has productivity of the user (teacher or administrator) improved? Is decision-making faster and more accurate because of the information provided by this system?

Accuracy: Are there fewer errors? Can school administrators rely more on this system than the old one?

Flexibility: Can the new system perform diverse instructional opportunities that were not possible before?

Reliability: Are there fewer breakdowns of this system compared with the previous one? Is uptime very high with this system? The reliability/uptime of an on-line network is probably the number-one criterion by which to judge its design and development.

Acceptance: Have both teachers and school administrators accepted the system?

Controls: Are adequate security and control mechanisms in place to prevent threats to the system such as errors and omissions, fraud and defalcation, data loss, breaches of privacy, natural disastrous, and the like?

Documentation: Does the system have adequate written/ pictorial descriptions documenting all of its hardware, protocols, software, circuits, and user manuals?

Training: Are training courses adequate, and are they offered on a continuous basis, especially for terminal operators? Are training manuals adequate and updated on a regular basis?

System Life: Is the life of the system adequate? When two to five years are spent designing and implementing a system, the system life should be of adequate duration to keep up with the technological changes.

It also may be advisable to evaluate your own performance during the design and development of this new network. In that case, examine such items as whether development time schedules were on target. Were development costs within budget, or was there a large cost overrun? Were any deviations from the original purpose/objectives and scope documented? Consider interactions with those affected by the system: Do they feel they were treated fairly, and are they satisfied with you and your design? Was there much turnover on the project team during the design and development?

Understanding the Current System

The object of this design effort step is to gain a complete understanding of the current operations and network (if any) that is functioning. This step provides a benchmark against which future design requirements can be established. It should provide a clear picture of the present sequence of operations, processing times, work volumes, current communication systems, existing costs, and user/management needs.

In order to be successful at this stage, begin by gathering general information or unique characteristics of the environment in which the system must operate. Next, identify the specific applications that use the data communication network and any proposed future applications.

Determine whether there are any legal requirements, such as local, state, federal, or international laws, that might affect the network. Consider the people in different departments who will be affected by the system. It is important to be aware that school district politics might affect the design effort; people may tell you what they want for their personal interests rather than what is in the best interests of the organization.

A written summary should be developed. This summary may include everything of importance learned during this step of the design. It is your written understanding of the existing systems. It should include any design ideas, notes on whether currently used forms or transmittal documents are adequate or inadequate, who was helpful or hindered progress, and any other impressions gained from interviews, meetings, data flow diagrams, flowcharts, sampling, and the like. In general, the written summary should contain information that can be referred to during the detailed design steps for development of the data communication network. It is the benchmark to be used for later comparisons.

Defining the System Requirements

The object of defining the general system requirements is to assemble an overview of the functions to be performed by the proposed network. At this point the input, processing, and output models for each of the application systems might be of great value.

During the early stages of defining the general system requirements, a review of the district's long-range and short-range plans is advised. This review helps provide the proper perspective in which to design a system that will not be obsolete in a few years and that will meet the future requirements of the district. These long- and short-range plans indicate such information as changes in organization goals, strategic plans, development plans for new programs, projections of enrollment growth, research and development projects, major capital expenditures, possible changes in curriculum, new services that must be served by the communication network, emphasis on security, and future commitments to technology.

Once the system requirements have been identified, they should be prioritized. That is, they should be divided into mandatory system requirements, desirable system requirements, and wish list requirements. This information enables the planners to develop a minimum level of mandatory requirements and a negotiable list of desirable requirements that are dependent on cost and availability.

Identifying the Geographic Scope

The scope of the application systems that are to be included on the network have been identified by now. The rough-draft geographic map that was developed during the feasibility study should be examined at this point, and a more detailed and accurate version should be prepared.

A data communication network has four basic levels of geographic scope:

— International (worldwide network).
— National (within the boundaries and laws of a single country).
— City (within the boundaries of a specific city, state/province, or local governmental jurisdiction).
— Local facility (within a specific district building or confined to a series of schools located on the same contiguous property).

At this point, identify the location of current telephone equipment rooms for incoming communication circuits (voice and data).

By the end of this task, there are tentative locations for individual terminals and circuit paths for the local facility, intracity, intrastate, country, and international needs.

Analyzing the Messages

In this step, each message type that will be transmitted or received from each application system at each terminal location is identified. Also, each message field (data item/attribute) is identified, along with the average number of characters for each field. Furthermore, it is necessary to identify message length and the volumes of messages transmitted per day or per hour. It may be necessary to visit each location where there is a system that will utilize the data communication network.

Each message should be described by a short title, and a sample of the message should be attached if there is a current equivalent. If there is not an equivalent, all of the fields that will make up the message must be identified. Message analysis sometimes reveals that the system will have to handle a greater volume of data than was previously thought.

The designers should plan for varying volumes at different hours of the day. For example, in an online connection, traffic volume peaks usually are in the midmorning. The network designer can calculate message volumes by counting messages in a current system or by estimating future messages. When possible, take a random sample for several weeks of traffic and actually count the number of messages handled each day at each location.

Calculating Traffic/Circuit Loading

Calculation of the circuit capacities is based on the number of characters per message and the number of messages transmitted per hour or per day. At this point, refer to the geographic maps and the pictorial diagrams of local facilities. Do these maps or pictorial diagrams still seem reasonable in light of the vast amount of further information that has been gathered during message analysis?

At this time, some of the maps or pictorial diagrams might be reconfigured slightly to further solidify the geographic configuration of the network. Remember to evaluate all the geographic maps: international, country, city/state, and local facilities.

The next step is to review all the network links over which data will travel. This may have been done when the network link traffic table was completed. If so, double-check to verify that each message type was cross-referenced to the proper network link.

To establish circuit loading (the amount of data transmitted), the designer usually starts with the total characters transmitted per day on each link, or if possible, the number of characters transmitted per hour if peaks must be met.

Starting with the total characters transmitted per day, the system designer first determines whether there are any time zone differences between the various stations.

Other factors to consider when evaluating line loading might be whether to include a message priority system. High priority messages may require special identification and, therefore, may increase the number of characters per message. If the message mix changes, and most messages become high-priority over a period of time, then more characters will be transmitted during a working day.

An inaccurate traffic analysis (confidence intervals) may also affect circuit loading. Try to account for any business operating procedures that might affect the system and the volume of data transmitted.

Finally, on the network maps and/or pictorial diagrams, begin recording some of the bits-per-second transmission rates that will be required for each circuit link. Sometimes it is useful to show the transmission capacity required for each link. Now add the bits per second transmission rate necessary for each circuit link. This helps when alternative network configurations, software, and hardware considerations are being developed and evaluated.

Developing a Control Matrix

Because the network probably will be the "lifeline" of the entire information flow within the school system, security and control are mandatory. All of the security and control mechanisms to be included in this data communication network must be taken into consideration during the design phase. As we stated earlier, we are well into an era in which information is the single most valuable resource within an organization. For this reason, it must be protected from all types of threats such as errors and omissions, message loss or change, disasters and disruptions, breaches of privacy, security/theft, unreliability, incorrect recovery/restart, poor error handling, and lack of data validation.

At this point, the network control matrix is developed. Review that section now to be sure you understand how to set up and continue development of this matrix through the remainder of the design project. At this time, develop the basic blank matrix, naming only the threats and components. As the design effort continues, identify controls and relate them to their threats and components by placing them in the appropriate cell of the matrix.

Determining Network Configurations

During this step of the system approach to designing a data communication network, the designer utilizes all the information collected to date. The network maps and the traffic/circuit loading data are of special value. These are used to configure the network in such a way as to achieve the required throughput at a minimum circuit cost. Begin this step by reviewing the maps and pictorial diagrams that show the links between the station/node locations.

The object of this step is to construct the circuit paths between users and the host computer. The decision involves moving the stations/nodes about, and making judgments with regard to software and hardware.

There is one other consideration in selecting the different network alternatives. The network designer must know whether the proposed alternative is going to maximize something, optimize something, or satisfy something, or if it will be a combination of the three. To maximize is to get the highest possible degree of use out of the system without regard to other systems. To optimize is to get the most favored degree of use out of the system taking into account all other systems; an optimal system does just the right amount of whatever it is supposed to do, which is not necessarily the maximum. To satisfy is to choose a particular level of performance for which to strive and for which management is willing to settle.

Now that the network maps/pictorial diagrams and traffic/circuit loading have been reviewed, line controls and modes of operation can be considered. This step involves choosing among various network alternatives. The main constraints are the availability of software packages, hardware, and circuit links. These three factors are all interconnected and must be considered along with the performance and reliability that must be obtained. All of these factors are also interrelated with regard to cost. Therefore, when alternative network configurations are developed, consider the software, hardware, circuits, performance, and reliability, and relate these factors to your cost/benefit analysis.

Software Considerations

With regard to software, the type of host computer may be a major constraint. The protocol the host can handle may limit the types of terminals or other hardware that can be utilized. This limitation may be eliminated through the use of protocol converters and/or the purchase of a new front end communication processor that can interface with the host and a variety of software and hardware.

The software will determine the line control methodology or mode of operation. Decide whether operations will be in full duplex or half duplex, asynchronous or synchronous, and at what speeds. The older byte-oriented protocols (such as Binary Synchronous Communications—BSC) probably are not a good choice because of their limitations on satellite links, slow half duplex operation, and inability to meet international standards. It is desirable to select a protocol that is compatible with the International Standardization Organization (ISO) seven-layer model, although reality might dictate that another protocol must be utilized in order to be compatible with existing hardware.

In addition to protocols/software, other network architectures or software that reside in the host computer and front-end communication processors have to be considered. For example, telecommunication access programs and the teleprocessing monitors may affect network operations. Security software packages in the host computer also can be a constraint. Finally, the host operating system itself may be a constraint to network control and operation, along with the database management system software.

Any software programs that are located out in the network should be reviewed. The network designer can make a major contribution to the future by selecting a protocol that can grow, that is compatible with an internationally recognized standard, and that will not have to be changed for at least five to ten years. The protocol is crucial because the host computer network architecture must be able to interface with it.

Finally, software diagnostics and maintenance must not be overlooked. Determine how quickly either in-house people or the vendor can diagnose software problems and how quickly they can fix these problems.

Hardware Considerations

Hardware that interacts with the alternative network configurations is easier to handle than software because hardware is a tangible item. These are some of the pieces of hardware that need to be considered:

— Terminals/microcomputers
— File servers
— Intelligent terminal controllers
— Modems (analog/digital)
— Multiplexers
— Intelligent multiplexers (STDM)/concentrators
— Line-sharing devices
— Protocol converters
— Hardware encryption boxes
— Automated switching devices
— PBX/CBX switchboards
— Data protectors
— Various communication circuit types
— Port sharing devices
— Front-end communication processors
— Host computers
— Testing equipment

With this in mind, the designer uses representations of the pieces of hardware and moves them about on the various network maps and pictorial diagrams. Experimenting with configurations, one should take into account the protocol/software considerations. The result should be a minimum-cost network that meets the school's data communication requirements. Many schools use computer simulation and modeling to carry out this task successfully.

Before ordering hardware, the design team should decide how to handle diagnostics, troubleshooting, and repair because hardware usually fails more often than software.

Network (Circuit) Costs

Usually, proposing cost limitations during the initial development of design alternatives is a hindrance. Of course, an effort always should be made to keep costs down; however, costs should not interfere with preliminary design configuration alternatives. Various alternatives should be identified first; then costs should be related to the attainable design configurations. The first task is to identify the attainable/workable configurations, and the second is to identify the costs of those alternatives.

Estimating the cost of a network is much more complex than estimating the cost of a new piece of hardware. Many variables and intangibles are involved. Nevertheless, estimating the cost of a system is a necessary prerequisite to deciding whether implementation is justifiable. Some of the questions that must be considered include the following:

• What are the major cost categories of the overall system? These may include:

> Circuit costs
> Hardware costs
> Software costs
> Maintenance/network management costs
> Personnel costs

• What methods of estimating are available and what accuracy can be achieved?

- Can all costs be identified and accurately estimated?
- Can benefits be identified? Which benefit can be estimated in dollar terms? Can they be measured in any other way?
- What criteria will management use when evaluating these estimates?

One of the alternatives to cost analysis is voice grade *circuit costs.* The major factors that have to be taken into account in figuring the cost of a voice-grade leased circuit include the circuit link mileage, cost (tariff) for the circuit, and any circuit termination charges at each end of the circuit link.

Selling and Implementing the Network

At this point there are two more subtasks:

— Sell the system both to the school administrators and to the teachers who will have to work with it. This is a verbal presentation.

— Implement the system. This probably is the most difficult task of all because the various pieces of hardware, protocol/software programs, network management/test facilities, and communication circuits must be assembled into a working network.

When presenting the system to gain management/user acceptance, the designer should be prepared for objections to the proposed system. Basic objections usually follow these lines:

— The cost is too high, or it appears too low for what the system is supposed to be able to do.
— The performance is not good enough, or it is more than is required at this time.

— The new network does not meet the goals, objectives, and policies of the district and schools that will be using it.
— The response or processing time is either too slow or too fast with respect to other operations within the organization.
— The system is not flexible enough. If changes are made in other areas, the network may collapse and the investment will be wasted.
— The quality, capacity, efficiency, accuracy, or reliability of the new network does not meet educational and/or district objectives.
— Certain school teachers and school administrators may dislike or distrust the network design team's motives, personalities, or presentation methods.
— You should review the list of evaluation criteria that was prepared earlier and be ready for questions on any that were not met.

The implementation process begins after the school administrator has accepted the new system. Implementation consists of the installation of the new system and the removal of the old system, if any. It involves hardware, protocols/software, communication circuits, a network management/test facility, people, written procedures that specify how each task in the network is performed, training, and complete documentation of the working system.

The steps involved in implementing a new data communication network can be developed to enable implementation to proceed as smoothly as possible The plan should specify who will do what and when they will do it. For this to be done properly, Gantt charts, flowcharts, the Program Evaluation Review Technique (PERT), or data flow diagrams should be used.

The design and implementation team must take into account the earliest lead times that are required to order hardware, software, and circuits. In many cases these items cannot be delivered immediately. In addition, some lead time is needed for testing the protocols and software to ensure that they operate in conjunction with the hardware and circuits. Both hardware and circuits may have to be implemented in various parts of the city, a state, throughout the country, or even internationally. For this reason, it is imperative that a decision is made as to how the new system will be implemented. Four basic approaches can be used:

— All at once. All nodes and the host computer are started up at the same time (a one-for-one changeover).
— Chronologically, and in sequence, through the system. Start with the first application system, implementing those portions of the network that must be implemented with it, and then move on to the second application system.
— In predetermined phases. Similar areas within the system are started up at one time, and other areas are started up later.
— Pilot operation. Set up a pilot or test facility (this later becomes one of the working nodes) to ensure that the operation is as expected before an all-at-once or chronological cutover is made.

Once the hardware is in place, the circuits have been installed, and the protocol/software is operating, training of the users can begin, although when possible it should be started earlier. Obtaining test terminals so that terminal operators can use their particular application system in a training/test mode months before they do so in real life is advantageous. Precise written procedures are required informing the terminal operators to operate the system for data input and manipulation. Written descriptions on how to retrieve and interpret the information output should be provided to the school administrators.

The training should include individual operator training, extensive written training manuals, and a methodology for continual updating of these manuals. At this point, the use of Computer Assisted Instruction (CAI) should be considered. With CAI, all of the training techniques and procedures are stored into the computer system; there are no written manuals. Instead, operators use their terminals for training as well as for standard business operations.

The network management/test center is a vital link in the network. This component must be in operation before the system is cut over to an operational status because reliability (uptime) is the single most important criterion for user acceptance.

Finally, after the system is operational, conduct follow-ups for the first six months or so to ensure that all parts of the new system actually are operating and that minor activities or operations have not been overlooked.

After the system is considered fully operational, reevaluate the network. Reevaluation may come 6 or 12 months later. It is a critical review of operator/user complaints, management complaints, efficiency reports, network management trouble reports, and an evaluation of statistics gathered on items such as errors during transmission and characters transmitted per link, and a review of peak load factors. Of course, it also should include a complete review of the original evaluation criteria so that you can determine the success of the design, development, and implementation of the new data communication network.

The above steps have been completed for the design of a new data communication system. Perhaps some steps can be omitted if a current network is being enhanced. For example, you might begin with "Analyzing Messages," or perhaps "Calculating the Traffic/Circuit Loading." It might be that your role involves nothing more than setting up a gateway to connect to public packet switching networks. If so, you might go directly to "Software Considerations" and "Hardware Considerations." The exact sequence of steps and the number of steps used are determined by the scope of the network design project. Even so, serious consideration should be given to all steps. As the project is closed, pull all of the documentation together and set it up in a binder that contains separate sections—one for each step that was carried out.

References

Blyth John and Blyth, Mary. (1985). *Telecommunications: Concepts, Development, and Management.* Mission Hills, CA: Glencoe Publishing Company.

Bracker, William E., and Sarch, Ray. (1985). *Case Studies in Network Design.* New York: McGraw-Hill Book Company.

DeNoia, Lynn. (1987). *Data Communication Fundamentals and Applications.* Columbus, OH: Merrill Publishing Company.

Fitzgerald, Jerry, and Ardra F. Fitzgerald. (1987). *Fundamentals of Systems Analysis: Using Structured Analysis and Design Techniques.* 3rd ed. New York: John Wiley & Sons.

Gaventa, William. (1990). *Cooperative Approaches to Respite Planning and Development.* (ERIC Document Reproduction Service No. ED 328008).

Green, James. (1986). *The Dow Jones-Irwin Handbook of Telecommunications.* Homewood, IL: Dow Jones-Irwin.

Rowe, Stanford. (1988). *Business Telecommunications.* 2nd ed. Chicago, IL: Science Research Associates, Inc.

Thomas, Ronald. (1984). *Telecommunications for the Executive.* Princeton, NJ: Petrocelli Books, Inc.

Chapter Ten

Telecommunications Management

Introduction

In the last 10 years telecommunications technology and regulatory environments have been changing so rapidly that most organizations are now taking steps to ensure that they are properly managing their communications facilities and people. An educational organization should understand some of the factors that have contributed to the increasing interest in communication management.

The goal of telecommunications management is to provide good telecommunications services for an organization and its employees at the lowest possible cost. Effective management of the telecommunications system requires a thorough knowledge of all aspects of the system and a way to measure system performance.

The responsibility of the manager is to become familiar with the existing system. The manager should be a key person in the establishment of organization telecommunications policy for providing telecommunications equipment and services, controlling usage, allocating costs to users, and training system users.

An Overview of
Telecommunications Management

Deregulation of the telecommunications industry has given organizations more choices and opportunities for communication services. But deregulation has brought with it the need for more analysis, judgment, and decision-making. Before deregulation, schools had only one choice for their telephone and data communications equipment circuits and services—the telephone company. Since deregulation, there are many competitive communications products.

Another factor in communication development is the technology that is making the integration of voice and data communications feasible. In the past, there was little overlap of the two and few possibilities for sharing services or facilities (such as circuits). Therefore, there was little incentive to manage the voice and data together. Today, telephones are being used as computer terminals, and voice is being digitized so that electronically it looks like data. Therefore, for many school districts, it is more feasible and desirable than ever before to group all communications activities together under one management.

Because of the increasing number of on-line, real-time computer systems and the growing number of computer terminals using those systems, many organizations must take a fresh look at what is being managed. In the past, most organizations viewed their department as having the responsibility of running a computer with terminals attached via communications lines. With the rapid increase in the number of terminals and personal computers, many of which are interconnected, schools are beginning to find that the operations department needs to focus primarily on running a communications network and communications can be a strategic asset to the educational system.

Data communications have developed within the data processing department. It is a much newer discipline because computer controlled data communications capabilities have only existed for a few years. In contrast with the relatively slow, steady growth of telephones, data communications has experienced an explosive growth as the use of terminals has blossomed.

Both the voice and data communications management have spent the last 25 years operating independently of one another. They have communicated with each other infrequently, if at all, installed separate networks of lines, and in some cases, offered competing capabilities or services to other departments. Clearly, there is synergism to be achieved by combining the management of voice and data communications facilities. While many data-function disciplines have not yet made this organizational change, there is a definite trend toward bringing the two together. The primary reasons for combining the two activities are efficiency, productivity, and cost advantage. With today's technology, communication circuits can be shared between voice and data; computerized PBXs require physical facilities like those that already exist in the mainframe computer room; redundant wiring in offices can be avoided; and the combining of staffs, equipment, and budget gives a communications manager more flexibility and opportunities for making trade-offs.

The Functions of the Telecommunications Department

Telecommunications organization has a certain set of responsibilities and activities to perform. Following are descriptions of the basic management functions that must be performed by the telecommunications department.

Design and Implementation of New Facilities and Services

All new communications facilities, including networks (both wide area and local area), building wiring, equipment, and services must be designed and engineered to meet specifications. Facilities and services should be designed in response to a statement of requirements based on the teacher's needs. Installation activities range from simple repetitive installation of new telephones and computer terminals to infrequent but complex tasks such as wiring a new building, installing a new PBX, a front-end processor, or a new version of the software. Because most of the work in the design and engineering section is project oriented, project management skills and techniques are important.

Network Operations and Technical Support

The network operations group is responsible for monitoring the status of the communications network and services, performing first-level problem solving when trouble occurs and monitoring communications service levels. The central telephone operators may also be included in this group.

The technical support staff provides a solution for the most difficult problems. They also perform software maintenance and assist with other telecommunications activities.

Administrative Support

The administrative support group provides primarily clerical support to the telecommunications department. They must be familiar with communications terminology and at least the general concepts of the network and equipment required, although detailed knowledge is not necessary.

The primary functions of the administrative support group include the following:

— Ordering/purchasing communications products and services.
— Receiving and identifying products when they are delivered.
— Conducting an inventory of all communications equipment.
— Checking, approving, and paying communications bills.
— Charging back for communications services rendered.

Many of these activities overlap with the work of other departments, including purchasing and accounting. These departments should agree on how much of the activity will be performed by the telecommunications administrative support people.

Other administrative activities are unique to the telecommunications department:

— Arranging for adds, moves, and changes of telecommunications equipment.
— Preparing and publishing the telephone directory.
— Registering new telecommunications system users.
— Training users in basic telecommunications operations.
— Maintaining telecommunications procedures.

Telecommunications Management Responsibilities

The basic responsibilities of general management can be applied to telecommunications management. These functions consist of:

— Staffing
— Organizing
— Planning
— Directing
— Controlling

Telecommunications management is unique in that only recently has the need to apply these management techniques to the telecommunications activity been recognized.

Staffing

A management function that is particularly challenging for communications managers is staffing the department effectively to accomplish the work to be done. Staffing is especially challenging because, for a number of years, there has been a shortage of trained, experienced communications people. Only recently have colleges and universities introduced programs focused on educating people for careers in telecommunications. Historically, the three primary sources of communications people have been from the telephone companies, the military, and internal people who learn telecommunications through on-the-job training.

Another complicating factor is the mix of skills required in the communications department. Planning, conceptualizing, operational, technical, and administrative skills are required by various members of the organization. When the department is small and has only a few people, it is difficult to obtain the right mix of skills. Larger districts have a better chance of obtaining people with the required skills or at least obtaining people with the aptitude to learn them. It may not be necessary for a telecommunications department to have all of the skills it needs. Outside consultants may be an effective supplement to the people within the telecommunications department, particularly when very specialized expertise is required. Typically, a telecommunications department staffing consists of:

The Telecommunications Manager

The telecommunications manager must be a conceptualizer and visionary as to how communications capabilities can be applied to solve problems. The school media specialist may be qualified for this responsibility. He or she must be articulate and persuasive, able to understand educational problems and opportunities, and able to envision how the application of communications technology might address these problems and opportunities.

Ideally, the manager (media specialist) will be included in high-level planning discussions with the school senior administrators to keep informed about the factors that are of importance to education and to ensure that the mission of the telecommunications department is lined up in support of those objectives. The manager needs to have an ability to grasp technical subject matter although he or she need not personally be a technician.

The telecommunications manager must be able to plan and implement projects at various scopes and levels. He or she must be a decision maker who can deal effectively with the educational problems of today and those of the future.

Designers and Implementers

Telecommunications network designers and implementers must have a good understanding of communications systems and product offerings. This knowledge is usually obtained through a combination of education and experience. Until recently, there were no college courses one could take to learn how to do this work.

Good designers are creative and innovative and have strong analytical skills. A knowledge of project management techniques is required. Network designers must also have good verbal and written communication skills. They work with eventual users of the system, as well as with the vendors who provide the equipment or services.

The school media specialist should actively be involved in the planning and implementation process and offer guidance on how to match the system with the educational objectives for creating a better and effective learning environment.

Network Operations Staff

Like many other professions, network operators often have contact with the users of the communications network. Therefore, they must be service oriented and strongly motivated to keep the network operational and performing properly at all times. Good verbal communications skills are required in order to deal effectively with the network users, many of whom experience problems with the network.

In addition to having good people skills, network operations people must thoroughly understand the network hardware and software that they are operating. There is a good deal of interchangeability between computer operations and network operations personnel. In most organizations, the ability to trade people back and forth is desirable, as it provides career opportunities for people in both groups.

The telecommunications and the data processing technical support people often have similar backgrounds and career paths. In many organizations, they are combined into a single technical support group.

Administrative Support Staff

The administrative support required in the telecommunications department is primarily clerical in nature. Experience with accounting and purchasing activities is desirable. A professional accountant may be required to ensure that proper accounting procedures are followed. The administrators need to be thorough and oriented in handling a mass of detail.

Often the administrative support personnel attend some specialized telecommunications courses to have a better understanding of the products and the services they are handling.

Staff Selection. In considering the telecommunications department staff, several questions need to be asked:

— Should experienced communications people be hired from the outside, or should current employees be trained in telecommunications skills and technologies?
— What career paths are available for communications employees? Will they be able to transfer to other functions within the company?
— Should some or all of the telecommunications work be contracted to outside firms? For what expertise should consultants be considered?

School administrators must recognize that because the telecommunications industry is growing rapidly, so is the market for good, experienced communications people, and salaries are high. When trade-offs must be made, it is normally better to select management people based on their skills and knowledge of educational telecommunications. The trade-off should be made in favor of specific telecommunications knowledge, experience, and education.

Use of Consultants. Every educational organization occasionally needs advice or assistance in areas where it has little or no expertise. In telecommunications, this is particularly true because of the rapid technological changes. Telecommunications managers may find that they need help evaluating a new technology such as fiber optics, or the impact of a new regulation or tariff. Sometimes a vendor can help with this evaluation, but since the vendor has a product to sell, the information he or she provides may be biased. AT&T has good network evaluation and design tools they make available to their customers, but obviously AT&T won't recommend a circuit provided by MCI or another carrier.

There are many telecommunications consultants in the field today. Some are independent, and some are associated with large consulting or public accounting firms. Before hiring a consultant, it is important to determine the consultant's expertise in the particular field of interest. It is important to ask other clients who have used the consultant about their opinions of the services provided. It is also important to find out exactly who will do the consulting work. The expertise and experience of the individual consultant is the primary determinant of the quality of the result, and it is important.

It is also important to define in writing the exact scope of the work to be performed and to ask the consultant for a written proposal and cost estimate, as well as a list of all of the items or documents that will be delivered at the end of the consulting period. The proposal can be used as an indicator of how well the consultant understands the educational domain. Some consultants may suggest modifications to the proposal, either to expand the scope of the work to be done or to reduce the scope to hold costs down. In any case, it is important to reach an understanding of the scope before any work begins.

Organizing

Organizing is the grouping of people to accomplish the mission of the department. The structure of the department is dependent on the sophistication and level of maturity of telecommunications in the school. As the school becomes more dependent on its telecommunications capability, the telecommunications department usually becomes larger and more structured in its operation.

One decision that the school administrator must make when organizing the telecommunications department is how much overlap there will be with other functions. For example, the telecommunications department needs a purchasing procedure, and the administrator must decide whether to set up its own purchasing group or use the school district's general purchasing department. Another decision is to determine which telecommunications activities are going to be performed by employees and which will be contracted to outside services or performed by vendors. Usually, ongoing activities such as communications operations are performed by school employees, whereas occasional work such as laying wires and cables is contracted to outside specialists.

As in any department, there are many ways to organize the people to carry out their responsibilities. The grouping of activities is typical of what is occurring in industry today, but is not the only possibility. While each telecommunications department has certain basic activities to perform, there is always flexibility to tailor the organization to the talents of its individual members.

Planning

In any organization, planning is required. The exact format and the frequency of the planning depends on the educational needs. Some school districts have very formal, detailed, rigorously scheduled planning procedures; other school districts operate on a less formal basis, putting plans together only when required.

Before looking at specific types of plans, it is important to point out that the telecommunications plan cannot exist in a vacuum; it must relate to the overall educational objectives. In most cases, telecommunications projects are not undertaken for their own sake, but are in support of some other activity within the school.

Long-Term Plan. The long-term plan should look three to five years into the future and give a vision of what telecommunications facilities and services will be required for the school and implemented in that time frame. Obviously, as a vision, it will never be 100 percent accurate but it is important to put this type of plan together to give a sense of direction. The five-year plan may show the need to explore communications options beginning in about three years, in preparation for the anticipated expansion to other areas.

The telecommunications manager often puts this plan together. He or she has the most contact with the senior administrator and others in the district. The long-term plan should be written, brief (10 to 15 pages at most), and as specific and pictorial as possible. It should be updated when needed (perhaps every year or two) to reflect changing educational strategies, new technological capabilities, and regulatory implications.

Medium-Term Plan. There should be a medium term plan covering a 6 to 18-month time period and identifying telecommunications projects and their priorities for that time frame. This plan should identify the financial and personnel resources needed to complete the projects in the plan, and the benefits that the implementation of the projects will bring to the school system. The medium-term plan should be tied to the budgeting process to ensure that money will be available to implement the projects listed in the plan. It should show the starting and ending dates for each project, but not the detailed tasks required for project implementation.

Like the long-term plan, the medium-term plan should be in writing. Each project listed in the plan should have information describing its scope, the reasons for implementation, its cost, benefits, starting and ending dates, and assigned personnel and equipment resources.

Project Plan. There is also a need for a specific task-oriented plan for each project, showing the tasks, worker days, cost, and people resources required to complete it. This plan should set targeted completion dates and identify responsibilities for each task. Detailed project plans should be updated as often as required. Depending on the size of the project, this may mean that monthly, weekly, or even daily updates are required. In any case, it is important to communicate changes to the plan and to all of the individuals involved in its implementation, as well as to users and management.

Regular reviews with the affected users and key management personnel are also desirable. Depending on the size of the project, reviews may be held weekly or monthly. These reviews help ensure that the project team is designing the telecommunications system correctly. The reviews also provide an opportunity to check progress and discuss any difficulties or unexpected circumstances that have arisen.

Directing

Management's responsibility for directing is to ensure that the mission and plans of the telecommunications organization are executed on a timely and accurate basis. This is best achieved by specifying the overall educational mission that is understood by the members of the group. Furthermore, each subgroup within the department must know its responsibility for helping to achieve the overall objectives.

Also, management must ensure that each individual is motivated and can see how his or her individual efforts help the department to meet its objectives and to be successful. To do this, specific objectives, goals, and standards of performance for each individual in the department are required. Objectives are frequently written annually, although there is significant benefit in reviewing and updating them more frequently. Other common techniques used in directing the department require each staff member to write a monthly report and hold project review meetings regularly. The purpose of both of these techniques is to improve communications within the department, as well as to allow individuals to gain recognition for the results they achieve.

Controlling

Unfortunately, the word controlling often has a negative connotation, but it simply means ensuring that performance is taking place according to the plans. Control activities are very important to any management process. Even the best made plans are subject to change. Part of managing is ensuring that changes in plans are done consciously and with a full understanding of the implications. In the telecommunications department, two major controls are financial controls and those applied to ensure the quality of the service being rendered.

Financial Controls. Financial controls take several forms. First, a financial plan or budget for telecommunications expenses is put together. Then performance against the budget is measured. In some school districts, telecommunications expenses are charged back to the schools when services are rendered. If this is the case, then chargeback rates must be established as a part of the budgeting process, based on the expenses which are expected to be incurred. By setting the chargeback rates higher than the project expenses, the telecommunications department becomes a profit center generating more income than it spends. If the charge-out rates are lower than the expenses, or if no charge-outs are used, then the telecommunications department is a cost center.

Expense Budgeting. Expense budgets are usually put together for the fiscal year used by the company; this may or may not correspond to the calendar year. First, the expenses for all existing people and communications facilities must be identified. Then all expected changes such as the addition of new people, circuits, or terminals must be identified and their costs added to the budget. Typically, the budget is broken into expense categories as described in the following list:

- Salaries—The total amount of money, including overtime, to be paid to employees in the department during the year.
- Employee Benefits—The amount of money to be paid for insurance, retirement, dental, and other benefit programs. It is often calculated as a percentage of the salaries and wages amount.

- Rental/Lease—The amount of money to be paid to vendors periodically for the use of equipment that has not been purchased.
- Maintenance—This amount of money is to be paid for the repair of equipment or for service contracts to cover the repair.
- Depreciation—Money budgeted to cover the depreciation expense for equipment that has been purchased.
- Supplies—Money in this category is for items such as ribbon and paper for printers, subscriptions to periodicals, general or special office supplies, and so forth.
- Training—Money budgeted for vendor classes, general seminars, and workshops.
- Travel—Money for the expenses of airline tickets, lodging, and meals for any trips.
- Utilities—Money to pay the heating, air conditioning, and telephone bills.
- Building/district overhead (sometimes called "burden")—Many districts assess a flat fee to each school for use of the facilities. This is sometimes expressed as an overhead rate, which may be based on the number of square feet occupied, the number of students in the school, or the size of the rest of the budget.

The telecommunications manager may budget for literally hundreds of items. Sometimes it is desirable to break individual budget categories into finer detail. A spreadsheet program operating on a microcomputer is an invaluable tool to use during the budgeting process. As additions or other changes are made to the budget, items can be added or numbers corrected quickly while the spreadsheet program recalculates the monthly and yearly totals instantly. Breaking the budget apart by months is desirable in order to easily account for items that are added or deleted in the middle of the year, and it also serves as a monthly milestone for checking actual expenses against the budget as the year progresses.

Capital Budgeting. In some school districts it is also necessary to prepare a capital budget. The capital budget is a plan for money to be spent on items that are purchased and become assets of the district. While conservative accounting practice dictates that as many items as possible are charged to current expenses, the Internal Revenue Service guidelines state that certain items with a long life must be capitalized (become assets) and their expense spread over the asset's life. This expense is recovered in the form of depreciation. When purchased (as opposed to rented or leased), most telecommunications equipment must be capitalized and depreciated.

A capital budget is a list of items to be purchased, their costs, expected useful life, and anticipated month of acquisition. Public school districts may have special capital expenditure authorization procedures beyond the budgeting process so that specific approval for each major capital purchase is obtained even though the budget had been previously agreed to.

Cost Control. During the month, invoices for installed equipment or new purchases come in from vendors. These invoices must be verified to ensure that the invoices are correct before they are submitted to the accounting department for payment. As the bills are paid, they are charged against the telecommunications department budget.

Periodically, it is necessary to check the total expenditures and compare them to the budget to ensure that costs are under control. Normally, reports are provided each month by the school district's accounting department. With this type of report and the appropriate detailed information to back it up, the telecommunications manager can keep close track of the money his or her department is spending and, if necessary, take appropriate steps to keep the expenses in line with the budget.

Chargeback. It is very common for some or all of the telecommunications expenses to be directly charged back to the users with some sort of a recharge system. All of the invoices for telecommunications equipment and services should pass through the communications department where they can be checked and approved by knowledgeable people. However, there is also a benefit in passing the costs on to the users of the communications system so that individuals realize that the service is not free. In most school districts, each school pays for its telephone equipment and long distance telephone charges through the internal chargeback system. It is also common for users of data terminals to purchase, or otherwise pay for, the terminal itself, and in many districts an internal bill for the use of the data network and other communications equipment is also generated. Many people believe that the only way to ensure that the costs of communications facilities are kept under control is to be sure that the each user is paying his or her own way. If there is a perception that communications services are free, they are more likely to be abused.

Quality Control. Telecommunications departments should have standards of performance for the services they provide. The standards should be agreed to among users and should meet their requirements. Typical standards set a level of expectations regarding network availability, response time, ability to obtain long distance lines, and so forth. Responsibilities must be assigned for monitoring and reporting performance against the standards and for making changes in the standards to address users' changing requirements. Typically, the network operations staff is responsible for this activity.

Telecommunications Audit. Another type of control is the periodic audit of the telecommunications activity by internal or external auditors. The purpose of any audit is to review the activities of a department to ensure that weaknesses in procedures or controls do not exist. Audits are normally conducted by individuals not involved in telecommunications and need not be limited to financial matters. Audits can also be used very effectively in the operations area to review existing methods and procedures for possible improvement. Typically, internal auditors report to a high-level administrator in the school district in order to maintain their independence from any department. Therefore, their reports usually require a formal response by the administrator of the department that has been audited.

Properly used, the telecommunications audit can be a very effective tool for checking the performance and upgrading the telecommunications activity. The audit provides an independent perspective of the operations and may provide valuable insights. If problems surface, they may give the manager some additional clout to get the problems corrected.

References

Bishop, Ann. (1990). *The National Research and Education Network (NREN): Promise of New Information Environments*. (ERIC Document Reproduction Service No. ED327219).

Castella, Donald. (1990). Career Networking—The Newest Career Center Paradigm. *Journal of Career Planning and Employment*, May, 32-39.

Fletcher, Patricia. (1990). Planning for the Future: The Leadership Role of the State Library Agencies. *Government Information Quarterly*, Winter, 403-414.

Green, James. (1986). *The Dow Jones-Irwin Handbook of Telecommunications*. Homewood, IL: Dow Jones-Irwin.

Kosiur, David. (1991). Managing Networks. *MacWorld,* February, 152-159.

Newsome, James. (1990). Environmental Scanning and the Information Manager. *Special Libraries*, Fall, 285-293.

Paris, Marion. (1990). A Management Survey as the Critical Imperative for a New Special Library. *Special Libraries*, Fall, 280-284.

Rowe, Stanford. (1988). *Business Telecommunications.* 2nd ed. Chicago, IL: Science Research Associates, Inc.

Saint-Germain, M. (1990). *Software Applications to Educational Planning and Management. A Collection of Papers.* (ERIC Document Reproduction Service No. ED 326205).

Chapter Eleven

Data Communication Security

Introduction

The ever-decreasing cost of hardware and software and an increasing quality and awareness of computer applications have generated a very high demand for computer acquisition and implementation among organizations in both public and private sectors. Many of these computers have been used or will be used in a network environment. It is estimated that over 90 percent of the minicomputers and mainframes sold or leased in the United States have communications capabilities. This could be the beginning of an increase in problems related to computer security. Computer security is no longer a technical problem. It is managerial as well as technical and this will have a dramatic impact on the success or failure of any computer utilization.

The National Center for Computer Crime Data (NCCCD), based in Los Angeles, reports that computer-related crimes were most often committed by programmers, students, and data entry operators. Exactly how the computer misdeeds are distributed is unknown. Studies by NCCCD, however, estimate that 44 percent of the computer crimes are money theft, 16 percent damage to software, 10 percent theft of information or programs, 12 percent alteration of data, and 10 percent theft of service.

Why Is Computer
Security Needed?

In an educational organization, information may range from employees' data to inventory data or even to sensitive student reports. This very expensive resource can be the target of unauthorized use such as divulging student records, changing grades, and possible destruction of a school's data file which would be disastrous for the organization.

When organizations decide to use computers, there are two options available. Option one prescribes a stand-alone system which is solely owned and used by a particular organization. If this is the case the security issues are more controllable.

Option two is the network utilization. This can be done using a timeshare system (one computer is used by several companies), a network system within the organization, or by networking with other public and private databases. Security problems are much more prevalent within the network environment. At the same time, more schools are becoming heavily involved in the networking environment. In today's complex educational environment, networking offers many unique advantages. Sharing the school's important information among the authorized personnel both inside and outside of the school's boundaries makes networking a viable alternative. Improved capabilities of networking systems and powerful and inexpensive microcomputers add to the attractiveness of the networking option. All of this indicates the importance of security measures in both public and private schools.

Types of Computer
Threats and Vulnerability

Before establishing a security system, school administrators must investigate and identify types and sources of computer threats. Generally speaking, computer threats can be classified as either acts of God or as man-made. Normal computer operation can be threatened by smoke, dirt, dust, corrosive material, illness of key personnel, resignation and strikes both inside and outside of the organization. Computer disaster can be caused by embezzlement (breach of trust) and fraud (deception by somebody not in a position of trust).

Some of these threats are controllable, some partially controllable, and some are totally uncontrollable. In any event, a security policy must be in place and must be known to all affected employees. Such a well-defined security policy will improve and expedite the recovery stage significantly.

Numerous computer threats can be caused internally. Table 11.1 summarizes types of threats and individuals who may cause such threats. Table 11.2 illustrates acts of God and man-made threats to a computer facility.

Table 11.1.
Source of Threats

Type of Threat	I/O Operator	Supervisor	Programmer	System/ Engineer Technician	User	Competitors
Changing codes	X		X			
Copying files	X	X	X			X
Destroying files	X	X	X	X	X	X
Embezzlement			X	X		X
Espionage	X	X	X			X
Installing bugs			X	X		X
Sabotage	X		X			X
Selling data	X	X	X		X	
Theft	X	X	X	X	X	X

Table 11.2.
Computer Disaster

Acts of God	Man-Made
Cold weather	Blackouts
Earthquakes	Fires
Floods	Gas leaks
Hot weather	Neighborhood hazards
Hurricanes	Nuclear attacks
Ice storms	Oil leaks
Ocean waves	Power failure
Severe dust	Power fluctuations
Snow	Radioactivity
Tornadoes	Structural failure

Security Measures

The first step regarding security protection is to generate back-up. Each working file must be fully backed up. The back-up process must take place on a regular basis. The back-up files must be kept in a different location than the computer room. Security measures can be classified in several different ways. Figure 1 illustrates types of security measures. There may be some overlap among the type of measures. Also, an organization may choose to implement one or several of these measures. Our classification includes general, physical, and software security. Figure 11.1 illustrates security measures.

General System Security

General system security includes biometric and non-biometric measures.

Biometric Measures

In recent years a series of biometrics have been used to protect the security of a computer installation. These include:

Fingerprint is used by scanning the user's finger. Whenever a user tries to access the system his/her fingerprint will be checked against the picture stored in a file.

Palm print in this type the individual characteristics of the palm are used as a source of scanning for identification purposes.

Hand geometry is done by using the length of the five fingers on each hand as well as the translucence of the fingertips and the webbing.

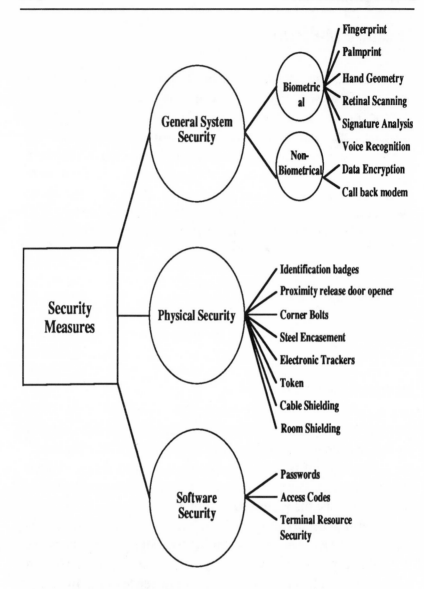

Figure 11.1. Security Measures. *Security measures can be divided into general system security, physical security, and software security.*

Retinal scanning is one of the most successful methods for security protection. In this type a scanning device is contained within a binocular eye camera. Identification is verified by the stored data on the user in a computer file.

Signature analysis uses the signature of the user as well as the user's pattern, pressure deviation, acceleration, and the length of the time which is needed for the user in order to sign his/her name.

Voice recognition translates words into digital patterns for transmission to the host computer. This technique is relatively new and more research is underway.

These different techniques have been very effective. They may not currently be financially justifiable. However, with rapid cost reduction and improvement in the quality, they present a viable alternative for the near future.

Non-biometric Measures

This type of security as the name indicates does not use biometric measures. Data encryption and call-back modems are two important security measures in this group.

Data Encryption is an effective security measure that can be installed in a computer system. The process of encryption entails the encoding of plain text into unreadable, scrambled text by a source cryptor which is located between the computer and the modem. Encrypted data is transmitted over a variety of transmission media such as phone lines, satellites, microwaves, coaxial cables, and fiber optic cables. Upon verification of the user, the data can be decoded into plain text. In the network environment encryption is becoming a common practice.

Call-back modem is another non-biometrical security measure. In this type the system tries to verify the validity of a
particular access by calling the user back.

Physical Security

Physical security primarily addresses the access control to
computers and the available devices which secure computers
from acts of theft. For the majority of organizations, physical
security is often the primary concern. The problem has been
continuously increasing with the growing use of microcomputers
in many executive offices. Physical security includes:

Identification badges, which are checked against a list of
authorized personnel. Checking must be done on a regular basis
so that any change in personnel will be noted.

Proximity-release door opener is an effective way to
control access to the computer room. Access to the computer area
is gained through the use of a small radio transmitter which is
located in the authorized employees' identification badges. When
authorized personnel come within a predetermined distance from
the entry door, a radio signal sends a key number to a receiver that
opens the door for their admittance.

Corner bolts are an inexpensive method of securing a
microcomputer to a desktop or counter. They include locks and
cables. Another method similar to corner bolts is the use of steel
bolts to secure micros to a heavy-duty locking plate which is then
bonded to an anchor pad that has adhesive on both sides and is
adhered to the desk or counter.

Steel encasement fits over the entire computer. The encasement is made of heavy gauge welded steel which is locked. The
security administrator or other designated person has control over
the key.

Electronic trackers are secured to the computer at the AC power insert point. If the power cord is disconnected, a coded transmitter sends a message to an alarm which sounds and/or a camera is activated to record the disturbance.

Token is a radio transmission device which is worn around the employee's neck. The device activates the computer when the employee is seated in front of the computer. After completion of the session the computer becomes inoperable.

Cable Shielding is accomplished by braiding layers of the conductors to become a braided shield. This scheme protects the data from any electronic leaks.

Room shielding is done by spraying a conductor material in the computer room. This material lowers the amount of signals being transmitted or can completely confine them within the room. A more expensive technique involves the shielding of the computer room walls with heavy sheet metal which keeps the high-frequency signals contained if there are any leaks.

Software Security

Software security is designed to protect the system from data integrity loss, unauthorized access, and to provide data security. Software security includes:

Passwords are one of the most basic of access controls. Passwords are sets of numbers, characters, words, or combinations that must be entered into the system for access. The length and the composition of the passwords determines their vulnerability to discovery by unauthorized users. The human element, which plays a major role in the success of the password control, is one of the most notable weaknesses of the password security system.

Access codes are the most basic security method. The simplest form of access control is the missing character code. Files and/or programs are listed in the directory incomplete. In order for the user to access the data, he/she must fill in the missing character(s).

Terminal resource security is a software capability which erases the screen automatically and signs off the user after a predetermined time lapse of activity. There are programs that allow users to access data for only certain time slots. Any attempt to access the system, other than the predetermined times, results in access being denied.

Viruses

In the late fall of 1987, a message went out from Lehigh University in Pennsylvania indicating that a computer specialist in the computer lab was busily fighting a virus program. The virus in question, dubbed the "Lehigh virus," spread itself from computer to computer using an infected disk as its mode of transmission. For a "clean" computer to be infected with this virus, it had to be booted up with an infected disk in drive A. Hundreds of computers were rapidly infected.

Computer viruses are very new in the United States; however, they have been around much longer in European countries. Virus infections also can be transmitted in a networking system causing the transfer of a virus from one computer to another computer at different sites. This is possible by using any communication line such as telephone, satellite, microwave, and so on. Probably the most dangerous type of virus infection would be from a bulletin board which can infect other members who access the bulletin board for sharing information. Some experts think that the greatest risk would come from infecting large computer networks such as those governing the air traffic controllers' system, the defense department, or NASA. Computer viruses have been observed in several countries including the United States, West Germany, Switzerland, Italy, Great Britain, and Israel. Computer viruses can be installed or programmed into a disk controller, hard disk, operating system or simply on a floppy disk.

The terms "virus" and "worm" showed up in science-fiction novels in the early 1970s. Around the same time, researchers at Xerox Corporation demonstrated a self-replicating code which they had created. They and other scientists hoped to use productive viruses as tracers and time-saving devices. But by the 1980s, viruses had escaped from computer-science laboratories and fallen into the hands of unprincipled programmers. Some programmers have modified other programmers' viruses to generate new strains, so there may be as many as 100 viruses in circulation by now.

Like a biological virus that takes over a living cell, a computer virus contains a set of coded instructions that enables it to invade a host, replicate, and infect new hosts. A sophisticated virus can spread undetected for a long time, waiting for a signal to begin destroying data. The triggers vary. For example, one common virus is programmed to wreak havoc only on Friday the 13th. Another comes to life after it has spawned four clones.

One thing all viruses have in common is that they are parasitic—they attach themselves to other programs. *Trojans* and *bombs*, two other forms of electronic vandalism that are sometimes called viruses, are not even self-replicating. A trojan, named for the famous Trojan horse of Greek history, is a program that seems harmless, but contains a malicious snippet of software. An unsuspecting user might try out a new computer game, for example, only to find that his hard disk has been reformatted during play. Bombs, which are similar to trojans, but need not be brought in from the outside, are also concealed in ordinary programs. A disgruntled employee, for example, might plant a "time bomb" scheduled to "explode" a month after he has been fired.

What does a virus do once it gets inside a computer? It can attach itself to the boot sector, the operating system, or an executable program. The boot is a start-up program that is loaded before any other software. It prepares the way for the operating system—a complicated set of instructions that controls the computer's operations and allows the user to run other software as well as devices like printers and modems.

A boot virus typically replaces the first track on a disk with part of itself. It then hides the rest of the virus, along with the real boot sector, somewhere else on the disk—an area that it marks as bad sector. The virus takes control whenever the machine is turned on; then it allows the original boot sector to do its work. Once in a machine, the boot virus copies itself onto the first sector of other disks that are inserted into the machine.

Viruses can also infect programs within the operating system, causing a variety of problems. The virus may infect files that are accessed, slow down the computer's functions, or alter messages that appear on the screen.

The most widespread viruses infect application programs—spreadsheets, word processors, games, and utilities. When these programs are executed, the viruses can spread to other hosts. Most viruses check to see whether a program has already been infected and avoid reinfecting files. Otherwise the programs will become too large to fit into memory, and the virus will be noticed.

Computers that communicate with other computers via telephone lines are very susceptible to viruses. An easy way to get infected is to copy a program from a computer bulletin board.

There are hundreds of these systems and many of their operators put software on-line without checking it for bugs. Personal Computing (1989) reported that Jet Propulsion Laboratory in California suffered four outbreaks of viruses in 1988. The problem was traced to software downloaded from bulletin boards.

The most publicized network-related disaster was the virus spread through government networks on November 1988 by a Cornell University graduate student. The virus paralyzed as many as 62,000 computers and caused about $96 million worth of damage. The virus destroyed no data but multiplied so quickly that it overloaded a series of networks across the country within hours of being planted. Had the virus been designed for maximum damage, it could have wreaked havoc on computer systems nationwide.

Essentially, a virus has four phases: the *dormancy phase* (optional), the *propagation phase*, the *triggering phase*, and the *damaging phase*. A propagation phase is all that is necessary for the program to be a virus; a virus does not have to cause damage. The creator of a virus might use a dormancy phase to instill a sense of trust in the user since the virus does not propagate or do damage during this phase. The triggering phase is launched by some occurrence, such as a certain date or a particular number of replications. Finally, the damaging phase does whatever harm the author intends the virus to do.

Some viruses even have a pre-trigger. This is a piece of code that lets the virus benignly sit in a program until something transpires, such as a particular date or time frame, the presence of another program or file, or the capacity of the disk exceeding some certain limit. Generally speaking, very few viruses have a pre-trigger.

If the virus doesn't have a pre-trigger, or if it does and its pretrigger goes off, then the virus or virus replication mode activates. At this stage, the virus replicates a virtual copy of itself into other programs or into certain system areas on the disk. When loaded and executed, each infected program or system area is a clone of the virus itself and will produce more clones.

Types of Viruses

Today, several major viruses are identified. Some of them are as follows:

LEHIGH
Origin: Lehigh University, Bethlehem, PA, Fall 1987.
Host: IBM PC's and compatibles.
Description: Infects command (.COM) file, increases file size by approximately 20 bytes, changes creation date and time, activates after four infections, and destroys all system data.
Symptoms: Changes in size of command (.COM) and loss of all data.

SCORES
Origin: Electronic Data System, Dallas, TX, Fall 1987.
Host: Macintosh.
Description: Infects any application program, increases program size by 7 kilobytes, seeks out new hosts at 3 1/2-minute intervals, creates invisible scores and desktop files, and looks for existence of specific file names for destruction.
Symptoms: Slowdown of system, problems with printing, system crashes, file size increases, and notepad and scrapbook icon modifications.

nVIR

Origin: Hamburg, West Germany, Summer 1987.

Host: Macintosh.

Description: Appears in many varieties, each with individual activation characteristics, places nVIR resource in system file, and once the system is infected, every application executed is infected.

Symptoms: Vary greatly because of the large number of varieties; system crashes, "beep" heard when an application is opened, with MacinTalk installed, the message "don't panic" is heard, and files disappear.

ISRAELI

Origin: Hebrew University, Jerusalem, December 1987.

Host: IBM PC's and compatibles.

Description: Infects any (**.COM**) or (**.EXE**) program's size by about 1.8 kilobytes, infected programs are modified to become memory-resident, programs are infected when executed in infected system, and floppy or hard disk can become infected.

Symptoms: General slowdown of the system, program disappears on Friday the 13th, (**.EXE**) files continue to grow in size until too large to execute, and available system memory decreases.

ALAMEDA

Origin: Merritt College, Oakland, CA.

Host: IBM PC's and compatibles.

Description: replaces original boot sector with itself, stores original boot sector on first free sector, infects through software reboot sequence, and does not flag original boot sector as unusable.

Symptoms: Slow boot sequence, system crash, and lost data.

PAKISTANI BRAIN
    Origin: Lahore, Pakistan, January 1986.
    Host: IBM PC's and compatibles.
    Description: Replaces original boot sector with itself, moves original boot sector to another location, adds seven sectors that contain reminder of virus, flags all modified sectors as unusable to protect itself, and replicates onto all inserted bootable floppies.
    Symptoms: Copyright© BRAIN label displayed on infected disk, slow reboot sequences, excessive floppy disk activity for simple tasks, and program crashes for some operating systems.

How to Disinfect Infection

    A variety of good antiviral programs are available, ranging from freeware to shareware to commercial programs costing many hundreds of dollars. There are many kinds of programs for different machines.

    Integrity checkers allows you to generate a unique signature or checksum for each program on your system. At boot-up time, these values are checked against the stored (and protected) copies. If there is a difference, you may have an infected program on your disk.

    Monitoring programs typically sit on the interrupts and examine each one that comes by for suspicious activity. If they notice something that the antiviral program's author thought was suspicious, they will interrupt the operation, trigger an alert of some sort, and ask the operator what to do.

    A subclass of these two classes is a program that monitors for a load-and execute instruction and does a checksum or signature check on the disk image of the program about to be loaded. If it has somehow changed from the stored value, the antiviral program triggers an alert.

Virus removers examine the hard disk for signs of viruses that the antiviral program's author knows about. If they find a program with the footprint of such a virus, at the very least, they will alert you to its presence. The better ones will also remove it.

Back-ups are the one defense against a virus, but they are not fail-safe. Some of the data might become corrupted by a virus, and the back-up sets of that data might also be infected You should run a virus checker after you have had to restore from a back-up.

Preventive Measures for Virus-Free Environment

Viruses are a serious problem, and they have the potential for becoming even more troublesome. Yet, with proper precautions, the computer might never be infected. To protect your microcomputers, use common sense and as many of the following preventive measures as you can.

— Run virus checks before backing up.
— Back up and archive more than just the most recent back-up. Assume that not only is your system infected, but so are your back-ups.
— Never work with original master disks. Write-protect them and make copies. Use the copies to install and run programs. This precaution cannot be emphasized enough. If you do not have uninfected original disks, you are not going to be able to replace applications that pick up a virus.
— Make a back-up copy of your uninfected System.
— Quarantine infected systems. Disconnect them from networks and don't move files from them until the virus is completely eradicated.

— Keep unfamiliar software on floppy disks until its quality
  is determined. The major bulletin boards have been
  quick to diagnose and eradicate any problems in their
  files. Still, it is in your best interest to be suspicious of
  all new downloaded software.
— If you're exchanging software with other users, be
  suspicious of all new programs.
— Don't be in a hurry to put new software on a hard disk.
  Run it from a floppy with the hard disk turned off. Some
  viruses contain time bombs and their effects may not
  show up right away.
— Record the sizes of the system and related files. The size
  of the system should not change unless you add or
  remove desk accessories or other resources. Record the
  size of a familiar application.

Guidelines for Comprehensive Security Measures

Security measures can be improved with moderate expense.
To establish a comprehensive security plan inexpensively, a
school can utilize its existing resources. The following suggestions should assist a school in setting some security guidelines.
— Organize a security committee. The committee will be
  responsible for:
  A. Setting the Security Policies and Procedures. A
     clear and precise network policy plays a significant
     role in an organization. Lack of such policies and
     procedures may result in engaging employees in unde-
     sirable activities which are not defined as wrong

conduct and, in turn, prevent the organization from prosecuting the computer abuser. Obviously, the policies and procedures should be reviewed and revised periodically to comply with the needs of the school.

B. Assessing the effect of system security in the school periodically.

C. Distributing passwords and account numbers.

D. Providing security training for key decision makers and computer users.

E. Establishing the necessary protection plan for the information system.

F. Developing a regular audit procedure for log-in and system use.

G. Obtaining employee and top management support for security policy enforcement.

H. Evaluating and revising the security policies constantly.

I. Labeling hardware and software with warning stickers.

J. Overseeing the security policy enforcement.

K. Designing of color-coded disks.

L. Advocating the use of paper shredders for computer wastepapers.

M. Designing an audit trail procedure for both input and output.

N. Designing a computer operation log to record the log-on and log-off times for different users.

O. Defining employee duties related to security enforcement.

P. Documenting and labeling all the hardware and software components.

— Post the organization's security policies in a visible place and/or in the front end of any entry port (log-in station). The signs should state the organization's policies on security.

— All employees must be sensitive to security problems.

— Keep personnel records and privileges up-to-date.

— Keep security codes strictly secret.

— Revoke terminated employees' passwords immediately so that a malicious employee cannot be destructive.

— Keep sensitive data, software, and printouts locked up to reduce the chance of accessing, stealing, or altering the information.

— Exit from the program/system promptly. Log off and turn off the computer. This would not allow an unauthorized access to the vulnerable files.

— Restrict the use of computer systems for certain application programs.

— Limit the employee access to the files to limit the system access chances.

— Limit computer access to authorized personnel only. Curious personnel will be kept away from the system.

— Consider unlisted telephone numbers. An unlisted number deters hackers and intruders to some degree.

— Compare the communication log against communication billing periodically. The log should contain all of the outgoing calls with the users' names and call destinations and time in and out. Also, keep a log of calls in and time in and out. The billing discrepancies should be investigated.

— Be prepared against computer virus by using anti-virus utility programs.

The above steps could be used as a guideline. Not every organization will need to implement every step; however, some may need to include even more steps to fit their needs.

What Do You Do If the Plan Fails?

As discussed earlier, the sources for computer threats are numerous, controllable, uncontrollable, or unintentional. In any event, schools must have a plan to respond to a disaster if it occurs. The response process known as disaster recovery planning system can play a major role in putting the organization back on its feet. The following steps must be taken before a disaster occurs and they may be of significant importance.

— Do back-up for all your computer files.
— Identify all the vendors and manufactures for all the software and hardware used in the organization. Record their most recent addresses and phone numbers.
— Document all the changes done to the initial hardware and software.
— Get a comprehensive insurance policy for your computer facilities.
— Use hot sites—separate computer facilities with all the needed equipment.
— Use cold sites—rooms with raised floors, air conditioning, and humidity control within the computer itself.
— Share ownership of back-up facilities.
— Use decentralized computer facilities.
— Arrange reciprocal agreements with other institutions.

References

Azarmsa, Reza. (1991). Computer Viruses and Safe Educational Practices. *Educational Technology*, November, 26-32.

Azarmsa, Reza and Bidgoli, Hossein. (1989). Computer Security: New Managerial Concern for the 1980s and Beyond. *Journal of Systems Management*, 21-27.

Azarmsa, Reza and Bidgoli, Hossein. (1988). Savvy Security Measures Keep Computer Intruders at Bay. *The Executive Educator*, June, 13-15.

Bidgoli, Hossein. (1989). *Decision Support Systems: Principles and Practice.* St. Paul, MN: West Publishing Company.

Bologna, Jack, (19880. News Briefs—Computer Virus Incidents Increase. *Computer Security Digest,* February, 1-2.

Bromley, Robert. (1988). Virus Protection for Microcomputer Systems. *Journal of Accountancy,* December, 123-126.

Evans, Sandy. (1986). What's New in Security Accessories. *Security Management,* January, 37-39.

Fish, Toni B. (1987). Are You Doing Anything? *Computerworld,* June 3, 23.

Gilbert, Jerome. (1989). Computer Crime: Detection and Prevention. *Journal of Property Management,* March/April, 64-66.

Greenberg, Ross. (1989). Know Thy Viral Enemy. *Byte,* June, 275-280.

Honan, Patrick. (1989). Avoiding Virus Hysteria. *Personal Computing,* May, 85-92.

Lyons, Daniel J., et. al (1988). Starve a Cold. Feed a Fever, Then Reboot. *PC Week,* January 19, 127.

McLellen,Vin. (1988). Computer Systems Under Siege. *The New York Times,* January 31, Section 3, Column 1.

Snyders, Jan. (1984). How Safe is Safe?" *Infosystems,* June, 64-65.

Stefanac, Suzanne. (1988). Mad Macs. *Macworld,* November, 93-101.

Stover, Dawn. (1989). Viruses, Worms, Trojans, and Bombs. *Popular Science,* September, 59-62+.

Appendix

On-line Educational Databases

There are numerous databases offering educational related information. Database vendors provide access to hundreds of thousands of bibliographic references. Several database vendors provide paid on-line access to information. Some of these vendors are:

BRS
BRS Information Technology
8000 Westpark Drive
McLean, VA 22102
(800) 289-4277

CompuServe
P. O. Box 20212
Columbus, OH 43220
(800) 848-8990

DIALOG
Dialog Information Services, Inc.
3460 Hillview Avenue
Palo Alto, CA 94304
(800) 334-2564

SpecialNet
GTE Educational Services
West Airfield Drive
P. O. Box 619810
D/FW Airport, TX 75261-9810
(800) 927-3000

The H. W. Wilson Company
950 University Avenue
Bronx, NY 10452
(800) 367-6770

Some of the databases are:

Abstracts of Instructional Materials/Abstracts of Research Materials (AIM/ARM). Describes instructional materials for vocational and technical education.
Vendor: DIALOG.

Bilingual Education Bibliographic Abstracts (BEBA). Citations and abstracts concerning language instruction, culture, and minority groups.
Vendor: BRS.

Comprehensive Dissertation Abstracts (CDI). Citations of dissertations on all topics. References are to Dissertation Abstracts International.
Vendors: BRS and DIALOG.

Ed-Line (EDL). Contains educational news, statistics and information; education public relations news and tips; a directory of on-line users; education exchange; and electronic mail.
Vendor: CompuServe.

Education Daily On-line (EDO). This database is a daily newsletter and covers federal, state, and local news about education policy, practice, funding, and research. Educational Daily also covers the national associations of educators, lawmakers, and administrators that play an important role in education policy. It includes detailed coverage of relevant federal and state courts, civil rights issues, and other legal issues in education.
Vendor: SpecialNet.

Educational Directory, Colleges and Universities. This database contains basic data on the location and characteristics of colleges and universities. Also included are data on accreditations and basic student charges.

Vendor: U. S. Department of Education, National Center for Education Statistics.

Education Index (EDI). This database indexes the key English-language periodicals in all areas of education. Areas covered include preschool, elementary, secondary, higher, adult, vocational, and continuing education. Other areas include educational administration and supervision, teaching aids and methods, curriculum and instruction, and physical and special education.
Vendor: The H. W. Wilson Company.

Educational Research Forum (EDRF). This database is intended for the use of educators and psychologists engaged in educational research. Files include: abstracts of conference presentations, drafts of articles or papers, assessment tools, statistics, minutes of association meetings, and transcripts of real-time conferences.
Vendor: CompuServe.

Education Resources Information Center (ERIC). Educational information including research, descriptions of exemplary programs, and journal articles. Each record contains a citation and an abstract of the article. Noncopyrighted articles are available in print or microfiche from ERIC.
Vendors: DIALOG and BRS.

Educational Testing Service Test Collection. This database contains descriptions and availability information on tests and assessment instruments in the following areas: achievement, aptitude, attitudes and interests, personality, sensory-motor skills, vocational-occupational areas, and tests for special population. It covers all age and grade levels.
Vendor: BRS.

Exceptional Child Education Resources (ECER). Citations and abstracts of articles concerned with the education of handicapped or gifted students.
Vendors: BRS and DIALOG.

National Center for Educational Statistics (NCES). Just about every educational statistic which is known can be found here. The NCES office does the searching and reporting for the cost of computer time. Vendor: Statistical Information Office, U. S. Department of Education.

National Information Center for Educational Media (NICEM). A listing of all types of nonprint instructional materials (films, slides, records, etc.) for all grades. Vendor: DIALOG.

National Information Center for Special Education Materials/ National Instructional Materials Information System (NICSEM/ NIMIS). All types of print and nonprint instructional materials for students with all types of disabilities. Vendors: BRS and DIALOG.

National Technical Information Service (NTIS). This database contains reports of government sponsored research on any topic. Vendors: BRS and DIALOG.

Research in Progress (RP). Research which is ongoing or recently completed is described in this database. Vendors: BRS and DIALOG.

Resource Organizations and Meetings for Educators (ROME). This database includes most of the organizations concerned with education and related disciplines as well as their meetings, projects and publications. Vendor: BRS

Resources in Computer Education (RICE). RICE provides information on educational software by subject, grade level, hardware, etc. Evaluation and producer information are also available. Vendor: BRS.

School Practices Information File (SPIF). This collection contains descriptions of the software, curricula, and in-service programs. Vendor: BRS.

Vocational Education Curriculum Materials (VECM). Another listing of print and nonprint materials for vocational and technical education.

Vendor: BRS.

U.S. Public School Directory (USPSD). Directory of the public schools in the nation including some demographic data.

Vendor: DIALOG.

Glossary

A

access control. Restriction of access to specified areas, equipment, or programs to authorized users only.

access line. A telecommunications line that continuously connects a remote station to a switching exchange. A telephone number is associated with the access line.

access method. Computer software that moves data between main storage and input/output devices.

acoustic coupler. Telecommunications equipment that permits use of a telephone handset to connect a terminal to a telephone network.

address. (1) A character or group of characters that identifies a data source or destination. (2) To refer to a device or an item of data by its address. (3) The part of the selection signals that indicates the destination of a call.

addressing. The means by which the originator or control station selects the unit to which it is going to send a message.

airline reservation system. An on-line application in which a computing system is used to keep track of seat inventories, flight schedules, passenger records, and other information. The reservation system is designed to maintain up-to-date data files and to respond within seconds to inquiries from ticket agents at locations remote from the computing system.

algorithm. A set of mathematical rules.

alphanumeric. Pertaining to a character set that contains letters, digits, and usually other characters, such as punctuation marks.

American National Standards Institute (ANSI). An organization formed for the purpose of establishing voluntary industry standards.

amplifier. A device that, by enabling a received wave to control a local source of power, is capable of delivering an enlarged reproduction of the wave.

amplitude. The size or magnitude of a voltage or current analog waveform.

amplitude modulation (AM). (1) Modulation in which the amplitude of an alternating current is the characteristic varied. (2) The variation of a carrier signal's strength (amplitude) as a function of an information signal.

analog signal. A signal that varies in a continuous manner. Examples are voice and music. Contrast with *digital signal*.

analog-to-digital (A/D) converter. A device that senses an analog signal and converts it to a proportional representation in digital form .

area code. A three-digit number identifying a geographic area of the USA and Canada to permit direct distance dialing on the telephone system.

ASCII. American Standard Code for Information Interchange. The standard code, using a coded character set consisting of 7-bit coded characters (8 bits, including the parity check), used for information interchange among data processing systems, data communications systems, and associated equipment. The ASCII character set consists of control characters and graphic characters.

asynchronous transmission. (1) Transmission in which the time of occurrence of the start of each character or block of characters is arbitrary. (2) Transmission in which each information character is individually synchronized (usually by the use of start elements and stop elements).

audio frequencies. Frequencies that can be heard by the human ear (approximately 15 hertz to 20,000 hertz).

audiotex A voice messaging system that can access a database on a computer.

authorization code. A code, typically made up of the user's identification and password, used to protect against unauthorized access to data and system facilities.

automatic answering. (I) Answering in which the called data terminal equipment (DTE) automatically responds to the calling signal; the call may be established whether or not the called DTE is attended. (2) A machine feature that allows a transmission control unit or a station to respond automatically to a call that it receives over a switched line.

automatic dialing. A capability that allows a computer program or an operator using a keyboard to send commands to a modem, causing it to dial a telephone number.

automatic teller machine (ATM). A specialized computer terminal that enables consumers to conduct banking transactions without the assistance of a bank teller.

B

background noise. Phenomena in all electrical circuitry resulting from the movement of electrons. Also known as *white noise* or *Gaussian noise*.

bandwidth. The difference, expressed in hertz, between the two limiting frequencies of a band.

bar code reader. A device that reads codes printed in the form of bars on merchandise or tags.

baseband. A form of modulation in which signals are pulsed directly on the transmission medium. In local area networks, baseband also implies the digital transmission of data.

baseband transmission. Transmission using baseband techniques. The signal is transmitted in digital form using the entire bandwidth of a circuit or cable. Typically used in local area networks.

batch processing. (1) Processing data or performing jobs accumulated in advance so that each accumulation is processed or accomplished in the same run. (2) Processing data accumulated over a period of time.

batched communication. A large body of data sent from one station to another station in a network, without intervening responses from the receiving unit.

Bell System. The collection of companies headed by AT&T and consisting of the 22 Bell Operating Companies and the Western Electric Corporation. The Bell System was dismantled by divestiture on January 1, 1984.

bid. In the contention form of invitation or selection, an attempt by the computer or by a station to gain control of the line so that it can transmit data. A bid may be successful or unsuccessful in seizing a circuit in that group.

binary. (1) Pertaining to a selection, choice, or condition that has two possible values or states. (2) Pertaining to the base-two numbering system.

binary code. A code that makes use of exactly two distinct characters, usually 0 and 1.

binary-coded decimal (BCD) code. A binary-coded notation in which each of the decimal digits is represented by a binary numeral, for example, in binary-coded decimal notation that uses the weights 8-4-2-1, the number 23 is represented by 0010 0011 Compare this to its representation in the pure binary numeration system, which is 10111.

binary digit. (1) In binary notation, either the character 0 or 1. (2) Synonym for *bit*.

bit rate. The speed at which bits are transmitted, usually expressed in bits per second.

bit stream. A binary signal without regard to grouping by character.

bits per second (bps). The basic unit of speed on a data communications circuit.

blank character. A graphic representation of the space character.

bridge. A device that allows data to be sent from one network to another so terminals on both networks can communicate as though a single network existed.

broadband. (1) A communications channel having a bandwidth greater than a voice-grade channel, and therefore capable of higher speed data transmission. (2) In local area networks, an analog transmission with frequency division multiplexing.

broadband transmission. A transmission technique of a local area network in which the signal is transmitted in analog form with frequency division multiplexing.

broadcast. The simultaneous transmission to a number of stations.

bypass. Installing private telecommunications circuits to avoid using those of a carrier.

byte. An 8-bit binary character operated upon as a unit.

C

call back. A security technique used with dial-up lines. After a user calls and identifies himself or herself, the computer breaks the connection and calls the user back at a predetermined telephone number. In some systems the number at which the user wishes to be called back can be specified when the initial connection is made and before the computer disconnects.

call control procedure. The implementation of a set of protocols necessary to establish, maintain, and release a call.

carriage-return character (CR). A format effector that causes the print or display position to move to the first position on the same line. Contrast with linefeed character

carrier system. A means of obtaining a number of channels over a single circuit by modulating each channel on a different carrier frequency and demodulating at the receiving point to restore the signals to their original form.

cathode ray tube (CRT) terminal. A particular type of video display terminal that uses a vacuum tube display in which a beam of electrons can be controlled to form alphanumeric characters or symbols on a luminescent screen, for example, by use of a dot matrix.

CCITT. Consultative Committee on International Telegraphy and Telephony.

cellular telephone service. A system for handling telephone calls to and from moving automobiles. Cities are divided into small geographic areas called cells. Telephone calls are transmitted to and from low-power radio transmitters in each cell. Calls are passed from one transmitter to another as the automobile leaves one cell and enters another.

central office switch. The equipment in a telephone company central office that allows any circuit to be connected to any other.

centrex. Central office telephone equipment serving subscribers at one location on a private automatic branch exchange basis. The system allows such services as direct inward dialing, direct distance dialing, and console switchboards.

character. A member of a set of elements upon which agreement has been reached and that is used for the organization, control or representation of data. Characters may be letters, digits, punctuation marks, or other symbols, often represented in the form of a spatial arrangement of adjacent or connected strokes or in the form of other physical conditions in data media.

check bit. (1) A binary check digit, for example. a parity bit. (2) A bit associated with a character or block for the purpose of checking for the absence of error within the character or block.

chip. (1) A minute piece of semiconductive material used in the manufacture of electronic components. (2) An integrated circuit on a piece of semiconductive material.

circuit. The path over which two-way communications take place.

circuit noise level. The ratio of the circuit noise to some arbitrary amount chosen as the reference. This ratio is normally indicated in decibels above the reference noise.

circuit-switched data transmission service. A service using circuit switching to establish and maintain a connection before data can be transferred between data terminal equipment (DTE).

circuit switching. The temporary establishment of a connection between two pieces of equipment that permits the exclusive use until the connection is released. The connection is set up on demand and discontinued when the transmission is complete. An example is a dial-up telephone connection.

clock. (1) A device that measures and indicates time. (2) A device that generates periodic signals used for synchronization. (3) Equipment that provides a time base used in a transmission system to control the timing of certain functions, such as sampling, and to control the duration of signal elements.

coaxial cable. A cable consisting of one conductor, usually a small copper tube or wire, within and insulated from another conductor of larger diameter, usually copper tubing or copper braid.

code. (1) A set of unambiguous rules specifying the manner in which data may be represented in a discrete form. Synonym for *coding scheme*. (2) A predetermined set of symbols that have specific meanings.

code conversion. A process for changing the bit grouping for a character in one code into the corresponding bit grouping for a character in a second code.

communications. (1) A process that allows information to pass between a sender and one or more receivers. (2) The transfer of meaningful information from one location to a second location. (3) The art of expressing ideas, especially in speech and writing. (4) The science of transmitting information, especially in symbols.

communications access method (CAM). Computer software that reads and writes data from and to communications lines. Synonym for *telecommunications access method (TCAM)*.

communications common carrier. In the USA and Canada, a public data transmission service that provides the general public with transmission service facilities; for example, a telephone or telegraph company.

communications network. A collection of communications circuits managed as a single entity.

communications standards. Standards established to ensure compatibility among several communications services or several types of communications equipment.

compression. The process of eliminating redundant characters from a data stream before it is stored or transmitted.

computer network. A complex consisting of two or more interconnected computing units.

concentration. The process of combining multiple messages into a single message for transmission. Contrast with deconcentration.

concentrator. (1) In data transmission, a functional unit that permits a common transmission medium to serve more data sources than there are channels currently available within the transmission medium. (2) Any device that combines incoming messages into a single message (concentration) or extracts individual messages from the data sent in a single transmission sequence (deconcentration).

Consultative Committee on International Telegraphy and Telephony (CCITT). An international standards organization that is part of the International Telecommunications Union, which is an arm of the United Nations.

control character. A character whose occurrence in a particular context initiates, modifies, or stops a control operation. A control character may be recorded for use in a subsequent action, and it may have a graphic representation in some circumstances.

control unit. A device that controls input/output operations at one or more devices.

controller. A device that directs the transmission of data over the data links of a network; its operation may be controlled by a program executed in a processor to which the controller is connected, or they may be controlled by a program executed within the device.

crosstalk. The unwanted energy transferred from one circuit, called the *disturbing circuit,* to another circuit, called the *disturbed circuit.*

cursor. (1) In computer graphics, a movable marker that indicates a position on a display space. (2) A displayed symbol that acts as a marker to help the user locate a point in text, in a system command, or in storage. (3) A movable spot of light on the screen of a display device, usually indicating where the next character is to be entered, replaced, or deleted.

D

data. (1) A representation of facts, concepts, or instructions in a formalized manner suitable for communication, interpretation, or processing by human or automatic means. (2) Any representations such as characters or analog quantities to which meaning is, or might be, assigned.

data circuit-terminating equipment (DCE). The equipment installed at the user's premises that provides all the functions required to establish, maintain, and terminate a connection, and the signal conversion and coding between the data terminal equipment (DTE) and the line.

data communications. (1) The transmission and reception of data. (2) The transmission, reception, and validation of data. (3) Data transfer between data source and data sink via one or more data links according to appropriate protocols.

data link. (1) The physical means of connecting one location to another to transmit and receive data. (2) The interconnecting data circuit between two or more pieces of equipment operating in accordance with a link protocol; it does not include the data source and the data sink.

data network. The assembly of functional units that establishes data circuits between pieces of data terminal equipment (DTE).

data PBX. A switch especially designed for switching data calls. Data PBXs do not handle voice calls.

data processing (DP). The systematic performance of operations upon data, for example, handling, merging, sorting, and computing. Synonym for *information processing.*

data processing system. A system, including computer systems and associated personnel, that performs input, processing, storage, output, and control functions to accomplish a sequence of operations on data.

data sink. (1) A functional unit that accepts data after transmission. It may originate error control signals. (2) That part of a data terminal equipment (DTE) that receives data from a data link.

data transfer rate. The average number of bits, characters, or blocks per unit of time transferred from a data source to a data sink. The rate is usually expressed as bits, characters, or blocks per second, minute, or hour.

dB meter. A meter having a scale calibrated to read directly in decibel values at a reference level that must be specified (usually one milliwatt equals zero dB). Used in audio-frequency amplifier circuits of broadcast stations, public address systems, and receiver output circuits to indicate volume level.

decibel (dB). (1) A unit that expresses the ratio of two power levels on a logarithmic scale. (2) A unit for measuring relative power. The number of decibels is 10 times the logarithm (base 10) of the ratio of the measured power levels; if the measured levels are voltages (across the same or equal resistance), the number of decibels is 20 times the log of the ratio.

decryption. Converting encrypted data into clear data. Contrast with *encryption.*

demodulation. The process of retrieving intelligence (data) from a modulated carrier wave; the reverse of modulation.

demodulator. A device that performs demodulation.

dial. To use a dial or push-button telephone to initiate a telephone call. In telecommunications, this action is taken to attempt to establish a connection between a terminal and a telecommunications device over a switched line.

dial back-up. A technique for bypassing the failure of a private circuit. When a failure occurs, a switched connection is made so that communications can be reinstated.

dial tone. An audible signal indicating that a device is ready to be dialed.

dial-up. The use of a dial or push-button telephone to initiate a station-to-station telephone call.

digital circuit. A circuit expressly designed to carry the pulses of digital signals.

digital signal. A discrete or discontinuous signal; one whose various states are pulses that are discrete intervals apart. Contrast with *analog signal.*

digital switching. A process in which connections are established by operations on digital signals without converting them to analog signals.

digital-to-analog (D/A) converter. A device that converts a digital value to a proportional analog signal.

direct current (DC) signaling. Signaling caused by opening and closing a direct current electrical circuit.

distortion. The unwanted change in waveform that occurs between two points in a transmission system. The six major forms of distortion are: (1) bias: A type of telegraph distortion resulting when the significant intervals of the modulation do not all have their exact theoretical durations; (2) characteristic: Distortion caused by transients that, as a result of the modulation, are present in the transmission channel and depend on its transmission qualities; (3) delay: Distortion that occurs when the envelope delay of a circuit or system is not constant over the frequency range required for transmission; (4) end: Distortion of start-stop teletypewriter signals. The shifting of the end of all marking pulses from their proper positions in relation to the beginning of the start pulse; (5) jitter: A type of distortion that results in the intermittent shortening or lengthening of the signals. This distortion is entirely random in nature and can be caused by such things as battery fluctuations, hits on the line, and power induction; (6) harmonic: The resultant presence of harmonic frequencies (due to nonlinear characteristics of a transmission line) in the response when a sine wave is applied.

distributed data processing (DDP). Data processing in which some or all of the processing, storage, and control functions, in addition to input/output functions, are situated in different places and connected by communications facilities.

distributed data processing network. A network in which some or all of the processing, storage, and control functions, in addition to input/output functions, are dispersed among its nodes.

downlink. The rebroadcast of a microwave radio signal from a satellite back to earth.

dumb terminal. A terminal that has little or no memory and is not programmable. A dumb terminal is totally dependent upon the host computer for all processing capability.

duplex. See *full-duplex (FDX)*.

duplex transmission. Data transmission in both directions at the same time.

E

EBCDIC. Extended Binary Coded Decimal Interchange Code. A coded character set consisting of 8-bit coded characters.

echo. The reversal of a signal, bouncing it back to the sender, caused by an electrical wave bouncing back from an intermediate point or the distant end of a circuit.

echo check. A check to determine the correctness of the transmission of data in which the received data are returned to the source for comparison with the originally transmitted data.

echo suppressor. A device that permits transmission in only one direction at a time, thus eliminating the problems caused by the echo.

electronic mail (E-Mail). The use of telecommunications for sending textual messages from one person to another. The capability to store the messages in an electronic mailbox is normally a part of the electronic mail system.

electronic mailbox. Space on the disk of a computer to store electronic mail messages.

electronic switching system (ESS). Electronic switching computer for central office functions.

encryption. Transformation of data from the meaningful code that is normally transmitted, called *clear text,* to a meaningless sequence of digits and letters that must be decrypted before it becomes meaningful again. Contrast with *decryption.*

error. A discrepancy between a computed, observed, or measured value or condition and the true, specified, or theoretically correct value or condition.

error correcting code. A code in which each telegraph or data signal conforms to specific rules of construction so that departures from this construction in the receive signals can be automatically detected, permitting the automatic correction, at the receiving terminal, of some or all of the errors. Such codes require more signal elements than are necessary to convey the basic information.

error correction system. A system employing an error detecting code and so arranged that some or all of the signals detected as being in error are automatically corrected at the receiving terminal before delivery to the data sink or to the telegraph receiver. Note: In a packet-switched data service, the error correcting system might result in the retransmission of at least one or more complete packets should an error be detected.

error detection. The techniques employed to ensure that transmission and other errors are identified.

error detecting code. A code in which each element that is represented conforms to specific rules of construction so that if certain errors occur, the resulting representation will not conform to the rules, thereby indicating the presence of errors. Such codes require more signal elements than are necessary to convey the fundamental information.

error message. An indication that an error has been detected.

error rate. A measure of the quality of a circuit or system; the number of erroneous bits or characters in a sample, frequently taken per 100,000 characters.

error ratio. The ratio of the number of data units in error to the total number of data units.

error recovery. The process of correcting or bypassing a fault to restore a computer system to a prescribed condition.

Ethernet. A local area network that uses CSMA/CD protocol on a baseband bus.

exchange. A room or building equipped so that telecommunications lines terminated there may be interconnected as required. The equipment may include manual or automatic switching equipment.

exchange code. The first three digits of a seven-digit telephone number. The exchange code designates the exchange that serves the customer.

extended binary coded decimal interchange code (EBCDIC). A coding system consisting of 256 characters, each represented by eight bits.

external modem. A modem that exists in its own box or cabinet.

F

facsimile machine (FAX). A machine that scans a sheet of paper and converts the light and dark areas to electrical signals that can be transmitted over telephone lines.

Federal Communications Commission (FCC). A board of commissioners appointed by the president under the Communications Act of 1934; the commissioners regulate all interstate and foreign electrical telecommunications systems originating in the United States.

flag. (1) Any of various types of indicators used for identification. (2) A bit sequence that signals the occurrence of some condition, such as the end of a word. (3) In high-level data link control (HDLC), the initial and final octets of a frame with the specific bit configuration of 01111110. A single flag may be used to denote the end of one frame and the start of another.

frequency. An attribute of analog signals that describes the rate at which the current alternates. Frequency is measured in Hertz.

frequency modulation (FM). Modulation in which the frequency of an alternating current is the characteristic varied.

front-end processor (FEP). A processor that can relieve a host computer of certain processing tasks, such as line control, message handling, code conversion, error control, and application functions.

full-duplex (FDX). A mode of operation of a data link in which data may be transmitted simultaneously in both directions over two channels.

full-duplex transmission. Data transmission in both directions simultaneously on a circuit.

G

Gantt chart. A project management tool that shows projects, activities or tasks (normally listed chronologically) on the left, and dates across the top. Each activity is indicated by a bar on the chart which shows its starting and ending dates.

gateway. The connection between two networks that use different protocols. The gateway translates the protocols in order to allow terminals on the two networks to communicate.

giga (G). One billion. For example, 1 gigahertz equals 1,000,000,000 hertz. One gigahertz also equals 1000 megahertz and 1,000,000 kilohertz .

Gray code. A binary code in which sequential numbers are represented by binary expressions, each of which differs from the preceding expression in one place only.

H

hacker. A term originally denoting a technically inclined individual who enjoyed pushing computers to their limits and making them perform tasks no one thought possible. Recently, a term describing a person with mischievous, malevolent intention to access computers in order to change or destroy data or perform other unauthorized operations.

half-duplex (HDX). A mode of operation of a data link in which data may be transmitted in both directions but only in one direction at a time.

half-duplex transmission. Data transmission in either direction, one direction at a time.

handset. A telephone mouthpiece and receiver in a single unit that can be held in one hand.

handshake. A security technique, used on dial-up circuits, which requires that terminal hardware identify itself to the computer by automatically sending a predetermined identification code. The handshake technique is not controlled by the terminal operator.

handshaking. Exchange of predetermined signals when a connection is established between two data set devices.

hertz (Hz). A unit of frequency equal to one cycle per second.

hierarchical network. A network in which processing and control functions are performed at several levels by computers specially suited for the functions performed; for example, in factory or laboratory automation.

high-speed circuit. A circuit designed to carry data at speeds greater than voice-grade circuits. Synonym for *wideband circuits.*

host computer. In a network, a computer that primarily provides services such as computation, database access, or special programs or programming languages.

hybrid network. A network made up of a combination of various network topologies.

I

identification (ID) characters. Characters sent by a station to identify itself. TWX, BSC, and SDLC stations use ID characters.

information bits. In data communications, those bits that are generated by the data source and that are not used for error control by the data transmission system.

information interchange. The process of sending and receiving data in such a manner that the information content or meaning assigned to the data is not altered during the transmission.

information resource management (IRM). An organization of the information-related resources of a company usually incorporating data processing, data communications, voice communications, office automation, and sometimes the company's libraries.

information security. The protection of information against unauthorized disclosure, transfer, modifications, or destruction, whether accidental or intentional.

integrated circuit. A combination of interconnected circuit elements inseparably associated on or within a continuous substrate.

Integrated Service Digital Network (ISDN). An evolving set of standards for a digital, public telephone network.

intelligent terminal. A terminal that can be programmed.

interactive. Pertaining to an application in which each entry calls forth a response from a system or program, as in an inquiry system or an airline reservation system. An interactive system may also be conversational, implying a continuous dialog between the user and the system.

interface. A shared boundary. An interface might be a hardware component to link two devices or it might be a portion of storage or registers accessed by two or more computer programs.

internal modem. A modem contained on a single circuit card that can be inserted into a personal computer or other device.

International Standards Organization (ISO). An organization established to promote the development of standards to facilitate the international exchange of goods and services, and to develop mutual cooperation in areas of intellectual, scientific, technological, and economic activity.

International Telecommunications Union (ITU). The specialized telecommunications agency of the United Nations, established to provide standardized communications procedures and practices.

J

jack. A connecting device to which a wire or wires of a circuit may be attached and that is arranged for the insertion of a plug.

jitter. Small, rapid, unwanted amplitude of phase changes in an analog signal. Small variations of the pulses of a digital signal from their ideal positions in time.

joy stick. In computer graphics, a lever that can pivot in all directions and that is used as a locator device.

K

key. (1) On a keyboard, a control or switch by means of which a specified function is performed. (2) To enter characters or data from a keyboard.

key-encrypting. A key used in sessions with cryptography to encipher and decipher other keys.

keyboard. (1) On a typewriter or terminal, an arrangement of typing and function keys laid out in a specified manner. (2) A systematic arrangement of keys by which a machine is operated or by which data is entered. (3) A device for the encoding of data by key depression, which causes the generation of the selected code element. (4) A group of numeric keys, alphabetic keys, and function keys used for entering information into a terminal and into the system.

kilo. One thousand. For example, 1 kilohertz equals 1000 hertz.

L

laser. A device that transmits an extremely narrow beam of energy in the visible light spectrum.

line. (1) On a terminal, one or more characters entered before return to the first printing or display position. (2) A string of characters accepted by the system as a single block of input from a terminal, for example, all characters entered before a carriage return or all characters entered before the terminal user presses the ATTENTION key. (3) See circuit.

link. A segment of a circuit between two points.

local area network (LAN). A limited distance network, usually existing within a building or several buildings in close proximity to one another. Transmission on a LAN normally occurs at speeds of 1 Mbps and up.

local central office. A central office arranged for terminating subscriber lines and provided with trunks of establishing connections to and from other central offices.

logical circuit. In packet mode operation, a means of duplex transmission across a data link, comprising associated send and receive channels. A number of logical circuits may be derived from a data link by packet interleaving. Several logical circuits may exist on the same data link.

log-off. The procedure by which a user ends a terminal session.

log-on. The procedure by which a user begins a terminal session.

long distance calls. Calls outside of the local service area.

M

main distribution frame. A frame that has one part on which the permanent outside lines entering the central office building terminate and another part on which cabling such as the subcarrier line cabling or trunk cabling terminate. In a PBX, the main distribution frame is for similar purposes.

mega. One million. For example, 1 megahertz equals 1,000,000 hertz. Also 1 megahertz equals 1000 kilohertz.

message. (1) An arbitrary amount of information whose beginning and end are defined or implied. (2) A group of characters and control bit sequences transferred as an entity.

metropolitan area network (MAN). A network of limited geographic scope, generally defined as within a 10-mile radius. Standards for MANs are being defined by the IEEE.

microcomputer. A computer system whose processing unit is a microprocessor. A basic microcomputer includes a microprocessor, storage, and an input/output facility, which may or may not be on one chip.

microprocessor. An integrated circuit that accepts coded instructions for execution; the instructions may be entered, integrated, or stored internally.

modem (modulator-demodulator). A device that modulates and demodulates signals transmitted over data communications lines. One of the functions of a modem is to enable digital data to be transmitted over analog transmission facilities.

modulation. The process by which some characteristic of one wave is varied in accordance with another wave or signal. This technique is used in modems to make DTE signals compatible with communications facilities.

modulator. A functional unit that converts a signal into a modulated signal suitable for transmission. Contrast with demodulator.

monitor. Software or hardware that observes, supervises, controls, or verifies the operations of a system.

multiplexing. (1) In data transmission, a function that permits two or more data sources to share a common transmission medium such that each data source has its own channel. (2) The division of a transmission facility into two or more channels either by splitting the frequency band transmitted by the channel into narrower bands, each of which is used to constitute a distinct channel (frequency division multiplexing), or by allotting this common channel to several different information channels, one at a time (time division multiplexing).

multipoint circuit. A circuit with several nodes connected to it.

N

network. (1) An interconnected group of nodes. (2) The assembly of equipment through which connections are made between data stations.

network addressable unit (NAU). In SNA, a logical unit, a physical unit, or a system services control point; it is the origin or the destination of information transmitted by the path control network.

network application. The use to which a network is put, such as data collection or inquiry/update.

network operator. A person or program responsible for controlling the operation of all or part of a network.

network topology. The schematic arrangement of the links and nodes of a network.

node. In a network, a point at which one or more functional units interconnect transmission lines. The term node derives from graph theory, in which a node is a junction point of links, areas, or edges.

noise. (1) Random variations of one or more characteristics of any entity such as voltage, current, or data. (2) A random signal of known statistical properties of amplitude, distribution, and spectral density. (3) Loosely, any disturbance tending to interfere with the normal operation of a device or system.

numeric keypad. Extra keys on a keyboard that function like a 10-key calculator.

O

off-hook. Activated (in regard to a telephone set). By extension, a data set automatically answering on a public switched system is said to go off-hook. Contrast with on-hook.

off-line. Pertaining to the operation of a functional unit without the continual control of a computer.

on-hook. Deactivated (in reference to a telephone set). A telephone not in use is on-hook. Contrast with off-hook.

one-way communication. Communications in which information is always transferred in one preassigned direction.

on-line. (1) The state of being connected, usually to a computer. (2) Pertaining to the operation of a functional unit that is under the continual control of a computer.

on-line system. A system in which the input data enters the computer directly from the point of origin or in which output data is transmitted directly to where it is used.

open network architecture (ONA). A set of provisions imposed by the FCC on the BOCs and AT&T to ensure the competitive availability of and access to unregulated, enhanced network services.

open wire. (1) A conductor separately supported above the surface of the ground; that is, on insulators. (2) A broken wire.

operating system. The central control program that governs a computer hardware's operation.

optical character recognition (OCR). The process of scanning a document with a beam of light and detecting individual characters.

optical recognition. A device that can detect individual data items or characters and convert them into ASCII or another code for transmission to a computer.

oscilloscope. An instrument for displaying the changes in a varying current or voltage.

overrun. Loss of data because a receiving device is unable to accept data at the rate it is transmitted.

P

packet. A sequence of binary digits (including data and call control signals) that is switched as a composite whole. The data, call control signals, and possibly error control information are arranged in a specific format.

packet data network (PDN). A network that uses packet switching techniques for transmitting data.

parallel transmission. (1) In data communications, the simultaneous transmission of a certain number of signal elements constituting the same telegraph or data signal. (2) The simultaneous transmission of the bits constituting an entity of data over a data circuit. Contrast with *serial transmission*.

parity bit. The binary digit appended to a group of binary digits to make the sum of all the digits either always odd (odd parity) or always even (even parity).

parity check. A redundancy check that uses a parity bit.

path. In a network, a route between any two nodes.

performance management. The application of management principles to ensure that the performance of a system meets the required parameters.

phase. An attribute of an analog signal that describes its relative position measured in degrees.

phase jitter An unwanted change in the phase of the signal.

phase modulation. Modulation in which the phase angle of a carrier is the characteristic varied.

picture element (pixel). (1) The part of the area of the original document that coincides with the scanning spot at a given instant and that is of one intensity only, with no distinction of the details that may be included. (2) In computer graphics, the smallest element of a display space that can be independently assigned color and intensity. (3) The area of the finest detail that can be effectively reproduced on the recording medium.

pixel. See *picture element*.

point-to-point circuit. A circuit connecting two nodes. Contrast with *multipoint circuit*.

polling characters. A set of characters peculiar to a terminal and the polling operation; response to these characters indicates to the computer whether the terminal has a message to enter.

port. An access point for a circuit.

private automatic branch exchange (PADX). A private automatic telephone exchange that provides for the transmission of calls to and from the public telephone network. See also *private branch exchange (PBX).*

private branch exchange (PBX). A private telephone exchange connected to the public telephone network on the user's premises.

private line. (1) A communications circuit that is leased from a common carrier. (2) A communications circuit that is owned by a company other than a common carrier.

private network. A network built by a company for its exclusive use using circuits available from a variety of sources.

program evaluation review technique (PERT). A project management technique that shows on a chart the interrelationships of activities.

propagation delay. The time necessary for a signal to travel from one point to another.

protocol. (1) A specification for the format and relative timing of information exchanged between communicating parties. (2) The set of rules governing the operation of functional units of a communications system that must be followed if communications are to be achieved.

protocol analyzer. Test equipment that examines the bits on a communications circuit to determine whether the rules of a particular protocol are being followed.

protocol converter. Hardware or software that converts a data transmission from one protocol to another.

public data transmission service. A data transmission service established and operated by an administration and provided by means of a public data network. Circuit-switched, packet-switched, and leased circuit data transmission services are feasible.

public network. A network established and operated by communications common carriers or telecommunications administrations for the specific purpose of providing circuit-switched, packet-switched, and leased circuit services to the public.

public switched network (PSN). A network that provides circuits switched to many customers. In the United States, there are four: telex, TWX, telephone, and broadband exchange.

public switched telephone network (PSTN). See *public switched network (PSN).*

public utility commission (PUC). An arm of state government that has jurisdiction over intrastate rates and services. Also known as public service commission (PSC).

pulse. A variation in the value of a quantity, short in relation to the time schedule of interest, the final value being the same as the initial value.

push-button dialing. The use of keys or pushbuttons instead of a rotary dial to generate a sequence of digits to establish a circuit connection. The signal form is usually tones. Contrast with rotary dial.

push-button dialing pad. A 12-key device used to originate tone keying signals. It usually is attached to rotary dial telephones for use in originating data signals.

Q

quadbit. A group of four bits. In 16-phase modulation, each possible quadbit is encoded as one of 16 unique carrier phase shifts.

queue. A line or list formed by items in a system waiting for service; for example, tasks to be performed or messages to be transmitted in a message routing system.

queuing. The process of placing items that cannot be handled into a queue to await service.

R

RS-232-C. A specification for the physical, mechanical, and electrical interface between data terminal equipment (DTE) and circuit terminating equipment (DCE).

RS-336. A specification for the interface between a modem (DCE) and a terminal or computer (DTE). This interface, unlike the RS232-C, has a provision for the automatic dialing of calls under modem control.

RS-44g. A specification for the interface between a modem (DCE) and a terminal or computer (DTE). This specification was designed to overcome some of the problems with the RS-232-C interface specification.

radio paging. The broadcast of a special radio signal that activates a small portable receiver carried by the person being paged.

rate center. A specified geographic location used by telephone companies to determine mileage measurements for the application of interexchange mileage rates.

receive-only (RO) device. A teletypewriter that has no keyboard. It is used where no input to the computer is desired or necessary.

relay center. A central point at which message switching takes place; a message switching center.

reliability. Trouble-free operation.

remote job entry (RJE). The process of submitting a job to a computer for processing using telecommunications lines. Normally the output of the processing is returned on the lines to the terminal from which the job was submitted.

repeater. A device that performs digital signal regeneration together with ancillary functions. Its function is to retime and retransmit the received signal impulses restored to their original shape and strength.

response time. The elapsed time between the end of an inquiry or demand on a data processing system and the beginning of the response, for example, the length of time between an indication of the end of an inquiry and the display of the first character of the response at a user terminal.

reverse channel. A means of simultaneous communications from the receiver to the transmitter over half-duplex data transmission systems. The reverse channel is generally used only for the transmission of control information and operates at a much slower speed than the primary channel.

ring. (1) The signal made by a telephone to indicate an incoming call. (2) A part of a plug used to make circuit connections in a manual switchboard or patch panel.

ring network. A network in which each node is connected to two adjacent nodes.

rotary dial. In a switched system, the conventional dialing method that creates a series of pulses to identify the called station. Contrast with *push-button dialing* and *dual-tone-multifrequency*.

S

satellite carrier. A company that offers communications services using satellites.

scrambler. A voice encryption device that makes the voice unintelligible to anyone without a descrambler, effectively rendering wiretapping useless.

screen. An illuminated display surface; for example, the display surface of a VDT or plasma panel.

serial. (1) Pertaining to the sequential performance of two or more activities in a single device. The modifiers serial and parallel usually refer to devices, as opposed to sequential and consecutive, which refer to processes. (2) Pertaining to the sequential processing of the individual parts of a whole, such as the bits of a character or the characters of a word, using the same facilities for successive parts.

serial system. A system made up of a number of components connected in series. In telecommunications, a terminal, modem, and computer may be connected in a series forming a serial system.

serial transmission. (1) In data communications, transmission at successive intervals of signal elements constituting the same telegraph or data signal. The sequential elements may be transmitted with or without interruption, provided that they are not transmitted simultaneously. (2) The sequential transmission of the bits constituting an entity of data over a data circuit. Contrast with *parallel transmission*.

shielding. A metallic sheath that surrounds the center conductor of a cable. Coaxial cable has shielding around the center conductor.

signal. A variation of a physical quantity, used to convey data.

signal-to noise ratio. The ratio of signal strength to noise strength.

signal transformation. The action of modifying one or more characteristics of a signal, such as its maximum value, shape, or timing.

signaling rate. The number of times per second that a signal changes. Signaling rate is measured in baud.

simplex circuit. Synonym for *one-way circuit*.

simplex communication. Synonym for *one-way communication*.

single mode. A type of optical fiber that has a glass or plastic core approximately 5 microns (.005 millimeters) in diameter.

sink. In telecommunications, the receiver.

smart terminal. A terminal that is not programmable but that has memory capable of loading with information.

source. The transmitting station in a telecommunications system.

specialized common carrier (SCC). Companies that offer alternative communications service to that of AT&T and the BOCs. Also known as *other common carrier (OCC)*.

star network. A network configuration in which there is only one path between a central or controlling node and each endpoint node. Synonym for *centralized network*.

start-stop transmission. (1) Asynchronous transmission such that a group of signals representing a character is preceded by a start element and is followed by a stop element. (2) Asynchronous transmission in which a group of bits is preceded by a start bit that prepares the receiving mechanism for the reception and registration of a character and is followed by at least one stop bit that enables the receiving mechanism to come to an idle condition pending the reception of the next character.

station. One of the input or output points of a system that uses telecommunications facilities; for example, the telephone set in the telephone system or the point at which the business machine interfaces with the channel on a leased private line.

step-by-step switch. A switch that moves in synch with a pulse device, such as a rotary telephone dial. Each digit dialed moves successive selector switches to carry the connection forward until the desired line is reached.

stop bit. In start-stop transmission, the bit that indicates the end of a character.

stop signal. (1) A signal to a receiving mechanism to wait for the next signal. (2) In a start-stop system, a signal following a character or block that prepares the receiving device for the reception of a subsequent character or block.

store-and-forward system. An application in which input is transmitted, usually to a computer, stored, and then later delivered to the recipient.

synchronous. (1) Pertaining to two or more processes that depend upon the occurrences of specific events, such as common timing signals. (2) Occurring with a regular or predictable time relationship.

synchronous transmission. (1) Data transmission in which the time of occurrence of each signal representing a bit is related to a fixed time frame. (2) Data transmission in which the sending and receiving instruments are operating continuously at substantially the same frequency and are maintained, by means of correction, in a desired phase relationship.

T

T-carrier system. A family of high-speed, digital transmission systems, designated according to their transmission capacity.

tariff. The published rate for a specific unit of equipment, facility, or type of service provided by a telecommunications carrier. Also, the vehicle by which the regulating agencies approve or disapprove such facilities or services. Thus, the tariff becomes a contact between the customer and the telecommunications facility.

telecommunications. (1) Any transmission, emission, or reception of sign, signals, writing, images, and sounds or intelligence of any nature by wire, radio, optical, or other electromagnetic systems. (2) Communication, as by telegraph or telephone.

telecommuting. Using telecommunications to work from home or other locations instead of on the business's premises.

telegraph. A system employing the interruption or change in polarity of direct current for the transmission of signals.

telephone company. Any common carrier providing public telephone system service.

telephony. Transmission of speech or other sounds.

teleprinter. Equipment used in a printing telegraph system.

teletex. A standardized communications messaging technology allowing automatic, error free transmissions between terminals at speeds 48 times greater than telex. Teletex is the logical successor to telex and TWX.

Teletype. Trademark of AT&T, usually referring to a series of teleprinter equipment such as tape punches, reperforators, and page printers that is used for telecommunications.

teletypewriter. A slow-speed terminal with a keyboard for input and paper for receiving printed output.

teletypewriter exchange service (TWX). Teletypewriter service provided by Western Union in which suitably arranged teletypewriter stations are provided with lines to a central office for access to other such stations throughout the United States and Canada. Both Baudot and ASCII coded machines are used. Business machines may also be used, with certain restrictions.

telex network. An international public messaging service using slow-speed teletypewriter equipment and Baudot code to exchange messages between subscribers. In the United States telex service is provided by Western Union.

terminal. (1) A device, usually equipped with a keyboard and a display device, capable of sending and receiving information over a link. (2) A point in a system or network at which data can either enter or leave.

time division multiplexing (TDM). A technique that divides a circuit's capacity into time slots, each of which is used by a different voice or data signal.

timesharing. (1) Pertaining to the interleaved use of time on a computer system that enables two or more users to execute computer programs concurrently. (2) A mode of operation of a data processing system that provides for the interleaving in time of two or more processes in one processor. (3) A method of using a computing system that allows a number of users to execute programs concurrently and to interact with the programs during execution.

token. A particular character in a token-oriented protocol. The terminal that has the token has the right to use the communications circuit.

toll. In public switched systems, a charge for a connection beyond an exchange boundary, based on time and distance.

tone signaling. Signaling performed by sending tones on a circuit.

topology. The way in which a network's circuits are configured.

touch-sensitive screen. A VDT screen that can detect the location of the user's finger using either a photosensitive or resistive technique.

Touchtone. AT&T's trade name for dual-tone-multifrequency dialing.

traffic. Transmitted and received messages.

transmission. (1) The process of sending data from one place for reception elsewhere. (2) In data communications, a series of characters including headings and texts. (3) The process of dispatching a signal, message, or other form of intelligence by wire, radio, telegraphy, telephony, facsimile, or other means. (4) One or more blocks or messages. Note: Transmission implies only the sending of data; the data may or may not be received.

transmission code. A code for sending information over telecommunications lines.

transmission control character. (1) Any control character used to control or facilitate transmission of data between data terminal equipment (DTE). (2) Characters transmitted over a line that are not message data but that cause certain control operations to be performed when encountered; among such operations are addressing, polling, message delimiting and blocking, transmission error checking, and carriage return.

transmission medium. Any material substance that can be, or is, used for the propagation of signals, usually in the form of modulated radio, light, or acoustic waves, from one point to another such as an optical fiber, cable, bundle, wire, dielectric slab, water, or air. Note: Free space can also be considered as a transmission medium for electromagnetic waves.

transmit. (1) To send data from one place for reception elsewhere . (2) To move an entity from one place to another; for example, to broadcast radio waves, to dispatch data via a transmission medium or to transfer data from one data station to another via a line.

trunk. A telephone channel between two central offices or switching devices that is used in providing a telephone connection between subscribers.

trunk group. Those trunks between two switching centers, individual message distribution points, or both, that use the same multiplex terminal equipment.

tuning. The process of making adjustments to a system to improve its performance.

twisted-pair wires. A pair of wires insulated with a plastic coating and twisted together, used as a medium for telecommunications circuits.

U

unipolar. A digital signaling technique in which a 1 bit is represented by a positive voltage pulse and a O bit by no voltage.

universal services. The attribute of the telephone system that allows any station to connect to any other.

uplink. The microwave radio signal beamed up to a satellite.

user response time. The time it takes the user to see what the computer displayed, interpret it, type the next transaction, and press the ENTER key.

V

value-added network (VAN). A public data network that contains intelligence that provides enhanced communications services.

videoconferencing. Meetings conducted in rooms equipped with television cameras and receivers for remote users' participation.

video display terminal (VDT). A computer terminal with a screen on which characters or graphics are displayed, and (normally) a keyboard that is used to enter data.

video signal compression. The process of reducing the number of bits required to carry a digitized video signal while maintaining adequate quality.

videotex. An application in which the computer is able to store text and images in digital form and transmit them to remote terminals for display or interaction.

virtual circuit. In packet switching, those facilities provided by a network that give the appearance to the user of an actual connection

virtual telecommunications access method (VTAM). IBM's primary telecommunications access method.

virtual terminal. A concept that allows an application program to send or receive data to or from a generic terminal. Other software transforms the input and output to correspond to the actual characteristics of the real terminal being used.

voice-band. The 300 Hz to 3300 Hz band used on telephone equipment for the transmission of voice and data.

voice compression. The process of reducing the number of bits required to carry a digitized voice signal while maintaining the essential characteristics of speech.

voice messaging. A messaging service that people use to leave voice messages for others. The system provides a voice mailbox on a computer in which the voice messages are digitized and stored. The voice equivalent of an electronic mail system for textual messages.

W

wide area network (WAN). A network that covers a large geographic area, requiring the crossing of public right-of-ways and the use of circuits provided by a common carrier.

wide area telecommunications service (WATS). A service that provides a special line on which a subscriber may make calls to certain zones using direct distance dialing. Charges for the service are a combination of a flat monthly charge and a usage charge.

workstation. The place where a terminal operator sits or stands to do work. It contains the working surface, terminal, chair, and other equipment or supplies needed by the person to do his or her job.

Index

V

VDT   116
very high frequency (VHF)   38
video display terminals
     (VDT)   114
video display units (VDU)   114
video terminals   114
videotex   4, 99
viruses   240
   damaging phase   243
   dormancy phase   243
   propagation phase   243
   triggering phase   243
virus removers   247
viruses, types of   244
   ALAMEDA   245
   ISRAELI   245
   Lehigh   244
   nVIR   245
   PAKISTANI BRAIN   246
   Scores   244
voice communication   2
voice mail   95, 96, 97
voiceband   61

W

WESTAR   26
Western Union   25, 26, 27
Westinghouse   30
WESTLAW   6, 7
white noise   62
wide area network (WAN)   110
workstations   6
worm   241
written message   2

SOURCE BOOKS ON EDUCATION